Puppets that are Different

AUDREY VINCENTE DEAN

illustrated by the author

TAPLINGER PUBLISHIN

First published in the United States in 1974 by
TAPLINGER PUBLISHING CO., INC. New York, New York

Printed in Great Britain

Library of Congress Catalog Card Number: 73-13436
ISBN 0-8008-6564-2

For Bob, with love

NOTE TO AMERICAN READERS

The following terms or references may be unfamiliar to American Readers of this book. Accordingly, short descriptions are supplied below:

broderie anglaise—edging ribbon with open embroidery
double crochet—American single crochet
furnishing fringe—drapery or upholstery fringe
guipure lace—a heavy patterned decorative lace with a flower motif
lurex—metallic fabric
press stud—snap fastener
stranded cotton—embroidery thread
wire wool—steel wool

Contents

A Word Before you Begin

PREPARING THE PATTERNS

Some of the patterns throughout the book are drawn on squared grids. Each square represents one inch either way. It is possible to buy paper already printed with one inch squares for redrawing dressmaking patterns, but you may prepare your own by ruling any firm paper with the required number of squares.

Copy the lines of the pattern from the diagram. This is easy if you redraw them square by square in the following way: begin anywhere and follow the outline in that one particular square, noting especially where it crosses the grid. Do the same in the subsequent square, and so on.

All the patterns are given to fit the average woman's hand or that of a child of junior to secondary school age. For a smaller or larger hand scale the pattern up or down slightly by drawing $1\frac{1}{4}$ in. squares for a larger puppet or $\frac{3}{4}$ in. squares for a smaller one. The amounts of material quoted will also have to be altered.

Actual size patterns only need tracing. Scribble lightly over the back of the traced lines and then put the tracing, scribbled side down, on to the paper. Redraw with a hard pencil in a different colour, to save accidental omissions.

Do not forget to copy on to your pattern any letters and dotted lines given in the diagram, as these will be used later in assembly of the pieces.

CUTTING OUT

All seam allowances on pieces which are to be cut in material other than felt have already been included in the pattern.

The usual amount given is $\frac{1}{2}$ in. but any variation is noted in the instructions. Oversewing on felt takes up so little that no seam allowance is needed.

If more than one pattern piece is to be cut in the same material, pin them all in place for a start so that you can judge the most economical way of cutting. Approximate quantities only are given in the patterns, and all yardages refer to 36 in. widths. The grain of the material should run straight up or across the pattern piece. Felt has no grain and the pieces can be juggled around as much as you wish for the least wasteful lay out.

Darts should be cut out completely, that is to say that the scissors should be guided into their slanting edges.

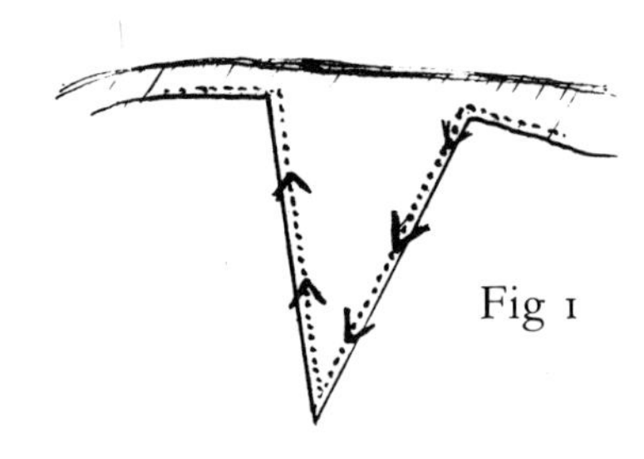

Fig 1

On some of the diagrams only half a pattern is given where it is identical on both sides. In these cases you may either draw half the pattern, allowing sufficient paper to fold it along the broken line and cut it out double, so producing the whole piece, or you may lay the half paper pattern along a fold in the material and cut the fabric double.

Should the fabric you are using have a right and a wrong side, remember to reverse the paper pattern when you need matching right and left hand pieces.

Before removing the pins transfer any assembly markings inside the pattern by two or three tailor's tacks, see figs. 2 and 3, or, if the marking is on the edge of the piece, by one or two over-sewing tacks. Corners and other obvious points do not need to be transferred but can easily be identified as work proceeds by a quick look at the pattern.

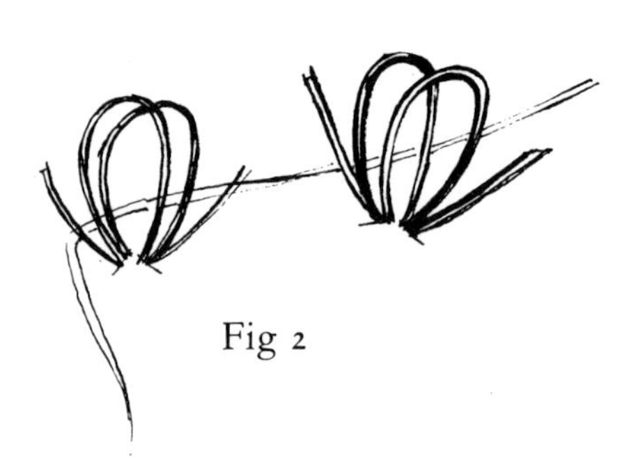

Fig 2

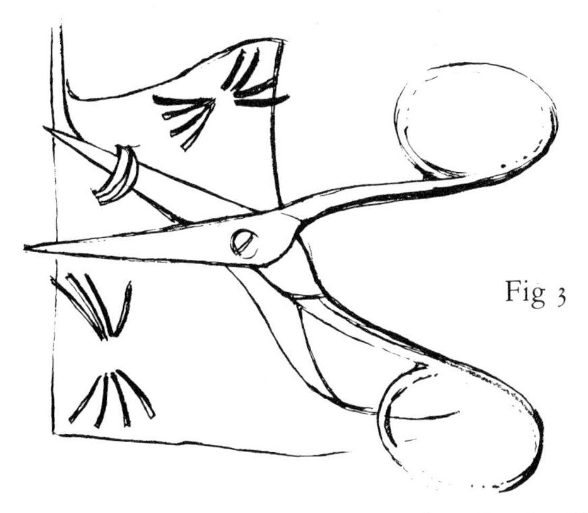
Fig 3

Fur fabric needs especial care. The pile should stroke in the direction shown by an arrow on the squared diagram. Use short small scissors for cutting out and take care to cut only the woven backing and not the pile of the material by sliding the scissors under the pile and taking short snips. In this way sufficient fur will be left to cover the seams.

TOOLS

A good selection of different needles is a help; crewel needles with long eyes, easy to thread with sewing or embroidery cottons; chenille needles, or larger knitter's needles, with large eyes and sharp points for wool; and extra long darners, useful for stabbing right through the puppet heads.

It is an asset to possess a large and a small pair of cutting-out scissors; also a pair of small electrician's pliers, with a pointed nose, for inserting glass eyes and pulling needle points through difficult places. Pipe cleaners are invaluable as a padded wire; other easily available wire is the brass picture-hanging kind, where one or more strands can be used as required.

Kapok makes the best stuffing and a small stick is helpful to push it into place.

SEWING

Before sewing, some pieces may be ironed on to commercial adhesive stiffening for fabrics. This gives a certain amount of extra firmness to individual pieces where it is required. Cut the same pattern in the stiffening; lay it on the back of the fabric, with the shiny side down, and press a hot iron on it to make it adhere.

Pin first, then tack should be the rule, especially when sewing by machine. To skimp on this step often means that the part slips out of place and will not fit correctly. Piecing is often more accurate if the pins are placed at right angles to the edge.

Darts are closed by matching the edges sloping into the point and oversewing them.

Felt can mostly be oversewn with small stitches on the right side. Use a fine needle for a regular finish. In some cases the felt may be edge stitched by machine for a neat appearance, as used on 'Goldilocks and the Three Bears'. In this instance the pieces should be accurately cut and tacked together, matching the edges carefully; stitch about $\frac{1}{4}$ in. away from the outline and then trim off any irregularities.

Woven fabric may be sewn by hand backstitch along the seam line; or machine stitching is unbeatable for speed and firmness wherever the seam can easily be negotiated. There is no virtue in hand stitching a toy if a machine will give accurate results. Ladderstitch is a useful way of closing all openings left for stuffing and of attaching ears and other features firmly and neatly. It is inconspicuous when complete. Use strong thread; take a small running stitch into one edge to be joined, then take another small running stitch in the other edge. Continue in this way, working into each alternately so that a line of neat vertical stitches will result in between to make a firm join.

Fur fabric should be first pinned together on the wrong side and then oversewn with a large stitch, tucking in the protruding pile with your needle as you work. Finally back stitch or machine stitch not more than $\frac{1}{4}$ in. from the edge. Do not remove the oversewing as it gives added strength and will neaten the inside. When the instructions state 'turn a narrow hem' it is often not necessary to turn the material more than once to the inside for about $\frac{1}{4}$ in.; oversew or herringbone down by hand, or stitch by machine, either with straight stitch or if possible with a zig zag.

INSERTING GLASS EYES

When you buy a pair of glass eyes you will find they are joined one on each end of a few inches of wire. Cut this with the pliers, leaving about $\frac{3}{4}$ in. behind each eye. Bend the wires over to form shanks like a shoe button with the point of the pliers. (Fig. 4, a.) Press the shank through the centre of the eye backing —you may need to make a tiny slit in the felt. Cut a length of strong buttonhole thread or fine string; thread it through the shank and tie a knot round it, bringing the ends together so that the thread is now double. (Fig. 4, b.) Pass the two ends through the eye

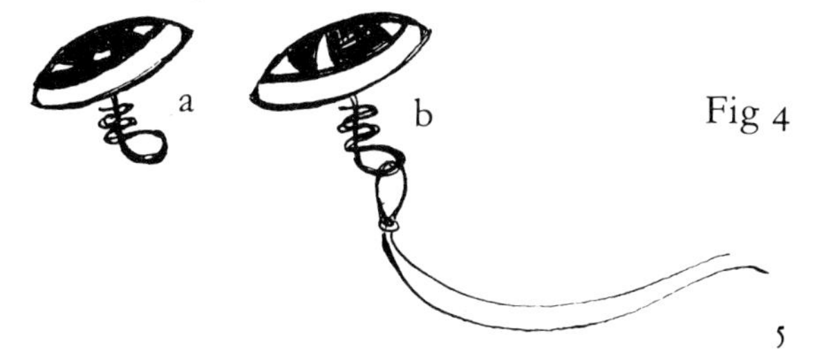

Fig 4

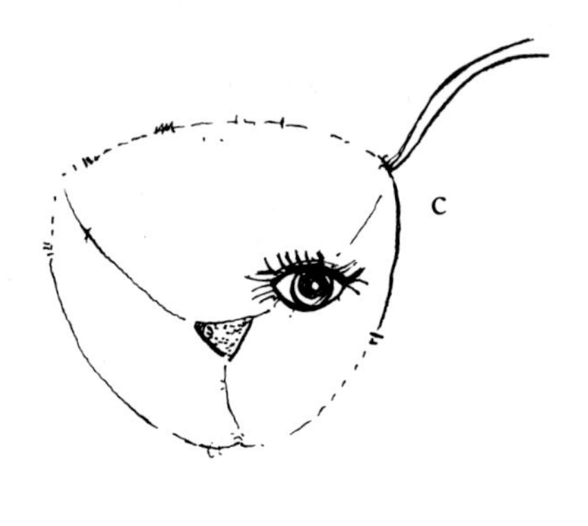

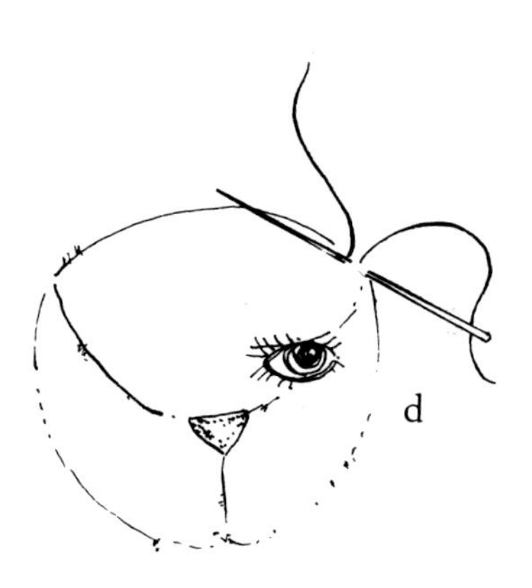

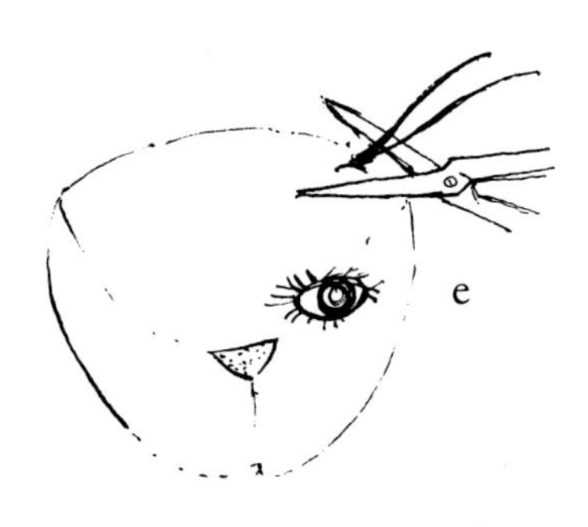

Fig. 4 continued

of an extra long darning needle. Stab the needle right through to the back of the neck or top of the head and pull the thread tight; thus sinking the eye well into the head. (Fig. 4, c.) Extract one end of the thread from the eye of the needle; take a small stitch with the other end; (fig. 4, d); then tie the two ends together firmly and cut the threads. (Fig. 4, e.) in some cases the ear may now be sewn over the knot. In others it will be found that a better result is achieved if the eye has been pulled towards the back of the neck. You will have to experiment a little. The felt eye backings are a valuable addition to glass eyes as they give extra colour and shape to the rather fishy appearance of the unadorned round button.

NEEDLE MODELLING

It is not always easy to achieve a good shape with your puppet's head simply through stuffing it, however judiciously. A little needle modelling will often pull it into a more interesting appearance. An extra long darner and strong matching thread are necessary. Take tiny invisible stitches right through the head from one point to another and pull tightly. The corners of felt eyes will benefit from this treatment and will be sunk more realistically into place. Sometimes the corners of mouths will also be improved. Animal heads, such as the kangaroo, may be easier to form if you consult a photograph or the coloured illustration while you shape them with a little needle modelling. Do not attempt to pull in round eyes such as those of the Baby in the Bed, where the effect to be aimed at is innocent doll-like simplicity.

USE OF ADHESIVE

Often a tricky small detail can be stuck with fabric adhesive, which is especially useful if the toy is quick and easy to make, and you know it is not intended to last long. However, when you have put a lot of work into a puppet it is a pity to skimp on the final effect, and sewing is preferable whenever possible to glueing: it lasts longer. Any fabric adhesives should be used as sparingly as possible, for a surplus often has a nasty tendency to yellow with age and seep unpleasantly through felt or fabric. A latex glue should be used with textiles; a clear all-purpose glue will stick sequins and glass jewels in place.

A dab of any adhesive is imperative on all knots and oversewings which hold some vital part, as for instance the Chirpy Chick's wings.

THE EFFECT TO AIM FOR WITH YOUR PUPPETS

Puppets are by their natures caricatures and are not in the least realistic. It is impossible to make a figure operated by the hand or by strings appear like an actor in miniature. So make a virtue out of necessity and enjoy the facts that you should aim at broad detail, with colour combinations in the main that are striking, and decorations that are noticeable for their telling appearance rather than for their painstaking handwork. Children enjoy gay colours and will accept anything, however improbable, if it is pleasing. Let yourself go: have a snake charmer made from mauve tights if this makes him look more sinister.

Suggestions only are given for colour schemes in the instructions and may be varied as much as you like. It is worth spending a little money on buying exciting material—after all, if you are prepared to devote time and trouble to your puppet, is not all your effort worthy of a little financial outlay?

A look round most department stores will show you felt in many shades, lurex and chiffon for mysterious or fearsome characters, and furnishing and dress braids of many kinds. At home collect odd bits of costume jewellery, any suitable dress making oddments, and outworn coloured tights—these are often invaluable for providing gauzy material and can be used double or treble thickness.

All the puppets in the book can be varied and suggestions are put forward for other ideas.

HAIR

Ways of creating a puppet's hair style are interchangeable.

1) Loose crocheted curls. These are most successful on a large scale puppet. With thick wool and a large crochet hook, make 1 chain. * Now work loop stitch thus:— hold wool on left hand in normal way but extend middle finger as far upwards as you can. Catch wool with hook on the further side of this finger and draw through loop on hook. Withdraw finger from loop you have just made round it; rearrange wool and make 1 normal chain. Repeat from * for length required.

2) Tight crocheted curls. *5 chain, 1 double crochet into 1st. chain; repeat from * for length required; sew in a spiral to head, starting from centre of crown. Suitable for Baby in a Bed.

3) Knitted curls. Cast on an odd number of stitches. Row 1:— knit. Row 2:—* Knit 1, insert needle into next stitch without knitting it, slip 2 fingers from left hand under point of right-hand needle, wrap wool round fingers and point of right-hand needle 3 times, draw loops through stitch on left-hand needle, slip sts. thus formed back on to left-hand needle, and knit all loops as one st.; slip the loops off the left-hand needle in the usual way; repeat from * to last st., knit 1. Row 3:— cast off.

Hair may also be suggested by straight stitches worked into the head for a close cut effect, or by loops of wool embroidered with a tiny backstitch in between each to stop them being pulled out of place. Several short lengths of wool can be backstitched in tufts to form ragged locks. Furnishing fringe, sewn in a spiral will give a taper cut hairstyle. Or make a wig, as directed in the instructions for the talking lion's mane on p. 20, but use a rather larger book, and sew it to the head with the line of stitching as the parting. Leave the strands loose or arrange and stitch them in a definite style. Bunches or ringlets can be suggested by winding folded pipe cleaners with some kind of yarn and then sewing the ends to the head underneath other strands of hair.

More suitable materials for coiffures include brass pan scrubbers, wire wool, which makes convincing iron grey waves, and synthetic raffia, available in all kinds of unnatural and stylish colours.

FEATURES

To develop your own ideas and to carry out successfully the designs in the book it is useful to know how to vary a puppet's facial features. Basically, a face without hair should be divided into thirds for an adult and halves for a child, with the features arranged as shown in fig. 5. Variations on these proportions will produce different effects. Keep the nose infinitesimal or not stated at all for a child and make the mouth either wide and cheerful or a rosebud-like spot, as shown in Goldilocks.

Fig 5

Fig 6

Eyes are great expression makers and emphasised eyelids also are most useful; see the kangaroo for its heavy eyelids. Fig. 6 shows varieties of eyes.

Noses can be left out altogether, as previously suggested, or they can be a round clownish knob, or you can copy the snake charmer's; a nose in a stuffed stocking face can again be made more pointed or bridged by inserting a suitably shaped piece of card under the fabric.

PAPIER MACHE

Finally, a word on papier maché—a very useful way of making accessories of all kinds. Some sort of armature or solid base should be selected for your work; it may be a cardboard cut-out or a round dowel, or a piece of wire, or pipe cleaners bent to shape. Tear up pieces of newspaper to the size of a postage stamp and stick them down layer by layer, using thin wallpaper glue or a paste made from a boiled solution of flour and water. The print can be alternate ways up on each layer so that you are able to see where you are in the thicknesses. The shape may be built up more quickly by winding paper kitchen towels, soaked in the glue, round the base you are using. Dry the finished article in a low oven, or stand it over a radiator or in an airing cupboard. When baked hard it can be sanded smooth exactly like wood. Paint with undercoat and then enamel, or use poster paints and then varnish.

Part One
Puppets with Moving Mouths

All these puppets have mouths which are operated by the thumb and forefingers of one hand. Their bodies extend over the forearm.

Sad Blue Hound Dog

This is one of the simplest types of puppet. You can vary the basic pattern of top and bottom head with a folded jaw in between as much as you like. Use orange with a few gold sequins and a bright pink jaw, hang the ears from the sides of the body as if they were fins for a talking gold fish. Make a cannibal from brown velvet with red lips and a scrap of fuzzy hair along the place where the Hound Dog's ears are sewn. Add brass ear rings and a bone thrust sideways through his nose. A pirate with a patch over one eye and a green lurex dragon also suggest themselves.

Materials
10 by 18 in. firm material such as felt, velvet or tweed; 7 by 9 in. contrast for mouth and ear linings; scraps of felt in ginger, orange, turquoise; 2 black beads or round domed buttons approx. $\frac{3}{8}$ in. diameter.

To Make
Cut patterns from squared diagram on p. 11. Actual size patterns for eyes, eye backings, nose and nose backings are given on the same page. Transfer ends of dotted lines and points B on top and bottom heads by means of tailor's tacks.

Head
Lay the patterns for the top and bottom heads along folds and cut 1 of each.

Cut a piece of felt or wool $1\frac{1}{2}$ by 2 in. and oversew it along the 2 longer sides to the wrong side of the bottom head, at the point indicated by the dotted lines. This will form a pocket for the thumb to control the lower jaw. Lay the right sides of the top and bottom heads together and join along the straight edges A to B on either side by oversewing if you are using felt, or by stitching $\frac{1}{2}$ in. from the edge if the puppet is being made in some other material. Turn in $\frac{1}{2}$ in. along the straight edge and stitch down. Felt will not need hemming.

Mouth
Cut 1 mouth in contrasting material. The dotted line B to B represents the fold at the corner of the jaw. Note that the upper mouth is larger than the lower. Still working on the wrong side, pin B on either side to points B of the heads. Join to the top and bottom heads by oversewing or seaming all round as before. Turn work to right side.

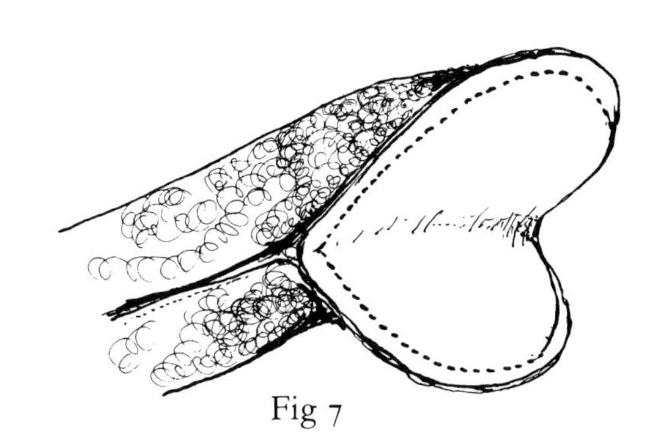

Fig 7

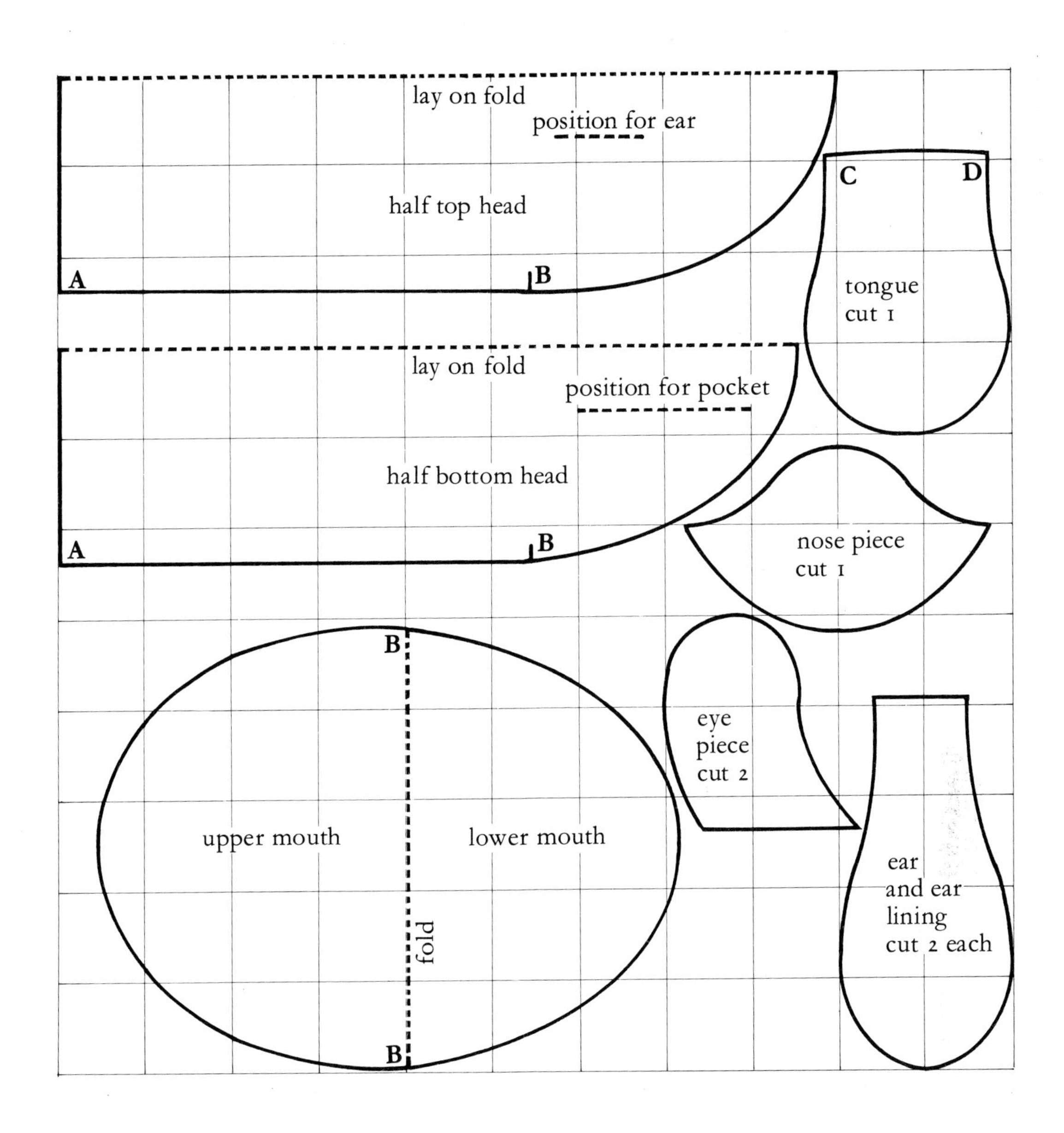

Actual size pattern

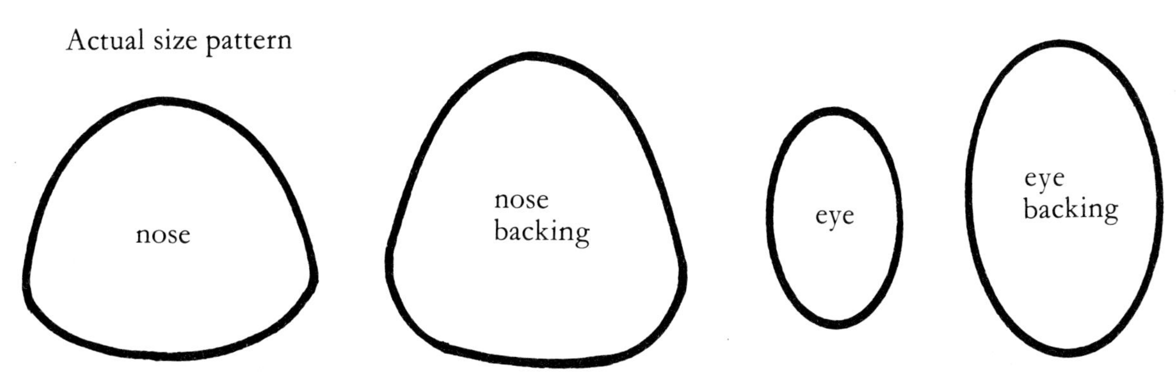

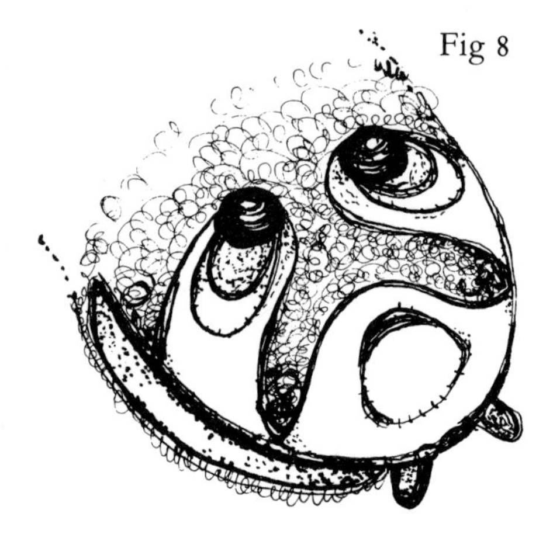
Fig 8

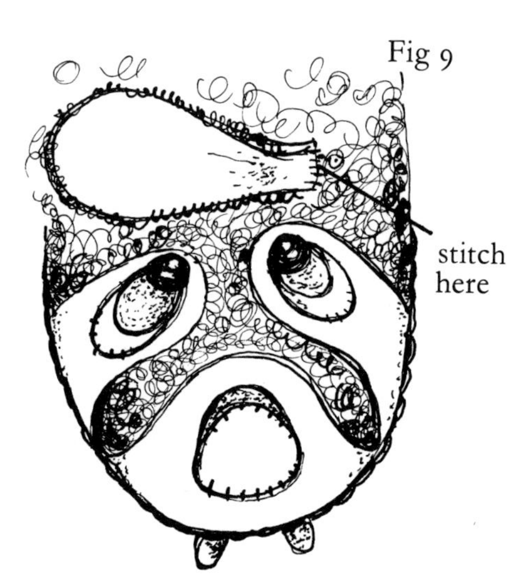

Fig 9

Features

Cut a nose piece and 2 eye pieces from ginger felt; cut a nose backing and 2 eyes from turquoise felt, and cut a nose and 2 eye backings from orange felt. Following the coloured illustration, sew the ginger pieces to the front of the top head, with the edges of each piece touching the mouth. Sew the blue nose backing to the nose piece, and the orange nose on top of it so that a curved strip of blue shows over the upper arched line. Sew the blue eyes over the orange eye backings with the black beads on top of them.

Cut 2 turquoise teeth, each about $\frac{1}{2}$ in. long by $\frac{3}{8}$ in. wide at the top, and sew them to the centre of the upper mouth at the join of the mouth to the top head. Cut a strip of turquoise 10 in. long by $\frac{1}{8}$ in. wide and catch it down to the upper mouth round the same curved join, over the top of the teeth.

Catch the ends C and D of the tongue together and sew the straight edges together for about $\frac{1}{2}$ in. Stick the tongue inside the lower mouth, with the sewn edges next to the material. Add a few stitches for security.

Ears

Sew an ear lining to the wrong side of each ear, leaving the straight edge open. Turn to right side. Sew to the top head on either side as indicated by the dotted lines on the pattern by first stitching an ear to the head, lining uppermost, as shown in fig. 9, then bend it over to hang away from the centre of the head. Catch down by a stitch or two from the lining to the head.

Loopy the Talking Lion & Harry the Talking Horse

These two puppets are rather more ambitious, but not difficult to make. They are both based on the same pattern.

Be adventurous with the colour scheme of the horse. Any fantastic combination will look well. This puppet may be used as the head of a hobby horse if you redraw the pattern on $1\frac{1}{2}$ in. squares and stuff it very firmly.

It would be easy to make a talking chimpanzee—give him a pink face and brown side heads. The ears are like those of a human and should be fastened to the sides of the head.

LOOPY THE LION

Materials

25 by 9 in. or 3 12-in. squares of orange felt; 4 by 5 in. red felt; 1 oz. double knitting or sport wool in rust; scraps felt in black, white, mustard, rust and cream; iron-on stiffening.

To Make

Cut pattern pieces from the squared diagram on p. 16. Patterns for the ears, nose, top nose and tongue are given actual size on pp. 16 and 17.

Cut face, 2 side heads and 4 ears from orange felt. Iron face, 2 side heads and 2 ears on to adhesive stiffening, reversing one of the side heads to make a pair.

With right sides together join centre back seam A to B and centre front seam C to D, either by oversewing or by machine stitching $\frac{1}{8}$ in. from the edge.

Features

Cut 1 face marking in cream felt, 1 top nose in mustard, and 1 nose in rust. For each eye cut 1 rust circle $1\frac{1}{4}$ in. diameter, 1 mustard circle 1 in. in diameter, 1 black circle $\frac{3}{4}$ in. in diameter. Stitching on the wrong side, close the small dart at the bottom of the face.

Oversew the face marking to the position indicated by the dotted lines in the squared diagram, using matching cotton. Alternatively the features may be edge stitched with black cotton as shown in the coloured illustration. Apply the nose top to the centre of the face, its straight upper edge coinciding with the top of the face. Place the nose on the end of the nose top. Stitch the rust eye circles to the face, then stick the mustard and black circles on top as shown in fig. 10. You may like to stick a gold sequin or small jewel to each eye.

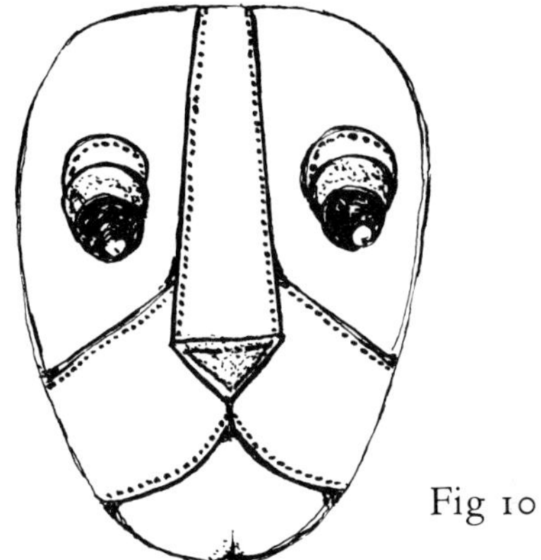

Fig 10

With right side to inside pin the centre of the nose top to point B of the centre back seam, and the edges of the face to the side heads, ending at point E on each side. Oversew the face to the side heads from E to E.

Mouth

Cut the mouth and tongue from red felt. Still working on the wrong side of the puppet, pin point F of the mouth to the small dart on the face, and G to point D of the centre front seam. Match the corners of the mouth to the corners of the jaw (points E at either side.) Oversew in place. Turn work to right side.

Lower Jaw Controller

Cut a piece of thin card 1 in. by about 4 in. and roll it widthways to fit the thumb loosely. Stick the ends, then stick a piece of felt round it and oversew the ends together. Smear fabric adhesive to the oversewn edges of the felt and slip the card and felt tube inside the puppet, placing the gummed part to the centre front seam inside the lower jaw. Working from the outside, take a few stitches along the centre front seam to hold the thumb controller firmly in place. (See fig. 11.)

Ears
Pin a stiffened and unstiffened ear together with the stiffening in between, and oversew round the upper edge. Sew 1 ear to the face on the seam between face and side heads, stitching it in the position indicated by H to I on the squared diagram. Finish the other ear in the same way.

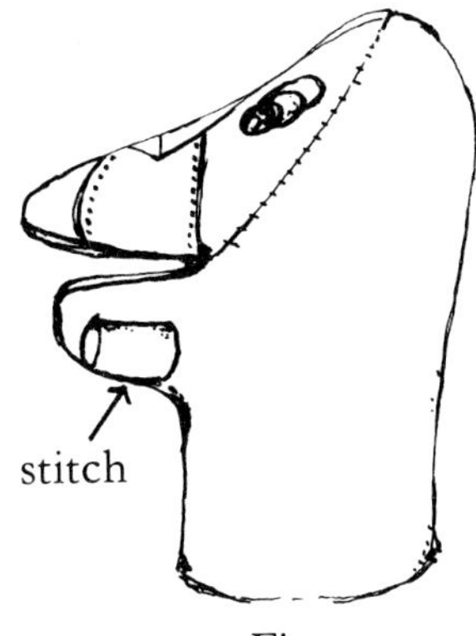

Fig 11

Mane
Cut a length of thin paper or newsprint approx. 18 in. long by 6 in. wide. Take a thin book measuring about 5½ in. from top to bottom of the cover, and wind some of the wool round this measurement. Cut the wool on each edge and lay the strands along the paper. Continue until all the wool is used and the paper covered. Now machine stitch down the centre of the strands through the paper and the wool. You will probably have to do this in stages, arranging the wool as you proceed. Remove the paper.

Fold the resulting fringe in half lengthways and oversew it to the lion, starting at the back of one ear and continuing round the face under the lower jaw. Cut off any surplus fringe and sew it to the forehead between the ears. Trim the mane so that it is about 1 in. long under the lower jaw.

Fig 12

Tongue
Cut the tongue from red felt and embroider a line of stem stitch in orange down the centre. With right side facing fold the 2 corners J and K to touch each other at the centre back, and catch the straight edges together for about ½ in. Stick the tongue inside the mouth so that it lolls out at one side (see coloured illustration), and fasten it firmly in place with a few stitches.

Teeth
Cut 4 pointed teeth from white felt, each about ⅝ in. long by about ⅜ in. wide at the top, and sew them to the jaw with about ½ in. space in between each one. Take a few white stitches along the spaces to link the teeth together.

HARRY THE HORSE

Materials
25 by 9 in. or 3 12-in. squares mauve felt; 7 by 7 in. bright pink felt; 1 oz. double knitting or sport wool in white; scraps felt in rose pink, white, purple, deep mauve, blue-green; 2 small silver-coloured bells; ¾ yd. ½ in. braid; ½ yd. cord; iron-on stiffening.

To Make
The horse is made in a similar way to the lion. Actual size patterns are given for the eyes, eye backings, tongue (the same as for the lion) and flowers for decoration.

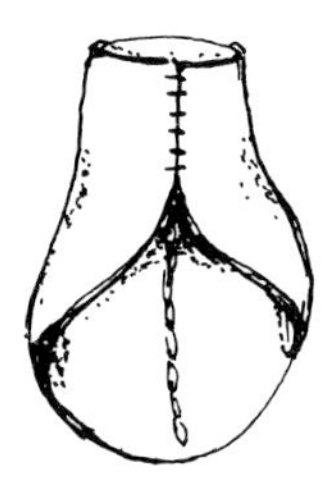
Fig 13

Ears
With the stiffening on the inside place a bright pink ear lining to a mauve ear and oversew round the slanted edges. L and M is the inside edge of each ear: ladder stitch each to the top corner of the head, in a similar position to the lion's ears, arranging the base of each ear in a curve.

Mane
The mane needs to be thick to give the best effect, so it should consist of a double thickness of fringe. Use 2 strips of paper each 12 in. long by about 6 in. wide, and following the instructions given for the lion's mane make two 12 in. lengths of fringe. Place one on top of the other and sew through the double thickness so that the mane starts on the puppet's forehead just between the ears, and ends at the bottom of the centre back seam.

Flower Decorations
Cut about 10 flowers to the actual size pattern in white, deep mauve, purple, bright pink and rose pink; and cut as many centres in the same colours. Stick them all over the horse at random, some colours overlapping others. Cut several pointed leaves in blue-green, about 1 in. long and ½ in. wide, and arrange them round the flowers.

Fig 16

Reins and Trappings
Cut a length of braid about 10 in. long, join short ends and position it round the horse's nose. Cut another 11 in. long and fasten it from the corners of the mouth around the back of the horse's head. Any suitable braid about ½ in. wide may be used: the horse in the illustration has trappings of purple felt stitched with green and edged with ric-rac in white.

The reins are a ½ yard of thick silky mauve cord, attached to the corners of the mouth. Sew a circle of green felt over these points where all the trappings meet and decorate them with small bells, one at either side.

Snake Charmer and Snake

This pair offers endless possibilities for striking colour schemes. If you could find a stocking with lurex in it for the snake so much the better. Look out your best glitter for the snake's eyes.

If some one can accompany the snake charmer on the descant recorder, a good tune to select is 'Temple Bells' from 'Four Indian Love Lyrics' by Amy Woodford Finden. Play it very slowly with lots of added twiddles. A record of Indian music would also be a good idea.

If your snake charmer's performance is only going to be operated by two people, one to play and one to work the snake charmer, he can have a snake made from beads attached by a fine invisible thread to the end of his pipe. Fasten the tail end of the snake to a small basket and let it slowly emerge.

SNAKE CHARMER

Materials

Old pair 20 or 30 denier tights, usual stocking colour; ½ yd. thin green lurex material; ¼ yd. thin turquoise lurex; scraps black net, acid pink chiffon, white felt, thin black cord; ½ yd. ½ in. wide silver braid; approx. 25 large pink paillettes; 2 ⅝ in. diameter black beads or buttons; 8 pipe cleaners; thin card; 6 in. length ½ in. dowel; kapok to stuff.

To Make

Cut the tights across the top of the thighs, on a level with the crotch, and keep both pieces.

Head

Cut a piece of thin card 3 by 6 in. and roll to fit the fore-finger loosely. Stick ends down. This is the inner tube for the head. Cut approx. 3½ in. from the toe end of one leg of the tights and fasten it over the tube, to prevent the stuffing of the head escaping.

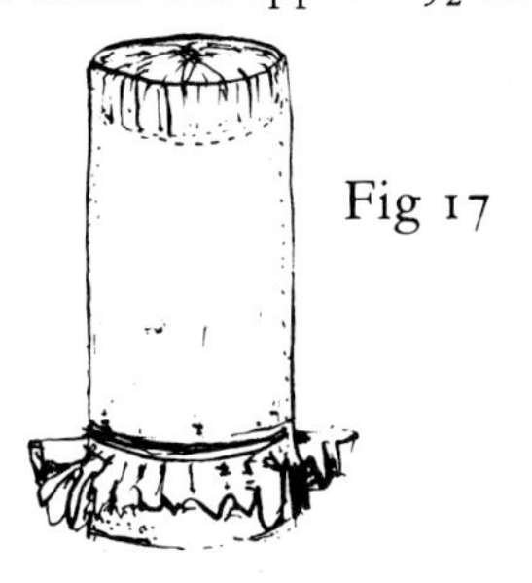

Fig 17

Tie a knot in the thigh end of one leg of the tights and cut across the stocking 6 in. below the knot. Put enough kapok into this bag so that it is roughly the size of a large grapefruit, about 15 in. circumference. The kapok should be well pressed together but should still retain a springy feel.

Push the inner tube into the stocking ball and fasten the stocking round the lower edge.

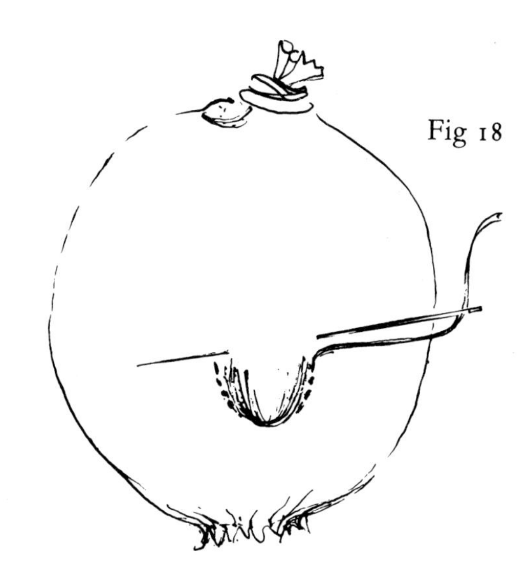

Fig 18

Tie a knot and cut off a similar amount from the other stocking leg. Pull it over the stuffed ball so that it is now covered by a double thickness of stocking.

The stitching is now added. You will need an 'extra long' darning needle and some matching strong sewing thread. Tie a knot at one end of the thread and take large stitches through the stocking and part of the stuffing inside. Pull the thread tight, take a tiny stitch in the surface and go back through the stocking. It is best to start by raising the nose.

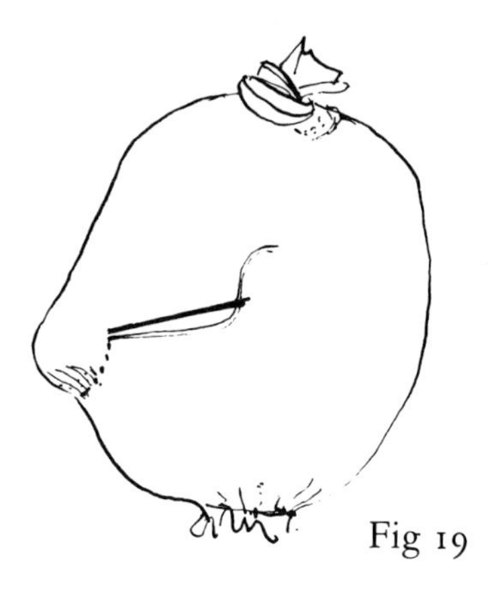
Fig 19

The process is easily carried out after a little experiment, and if the results are not as you expect it is simple to remove and reinsert the stitches. Gather across the mouth to give a puckered appearance and pull in deep set eye cavities. You can raise high cheek bones, and gather as much as you like to produce wrinkles.

Now stick the beads or buttons into the eyes, with scraps of white felt for the whites.

Cut several lengths of black cord for the drooping moustache; the longest should be about 4 in. and the shortest about 2 in.; bind them together round the middle and sew under the nose. Stick or stitch several short lengths of cord to represent thick beetling brows.

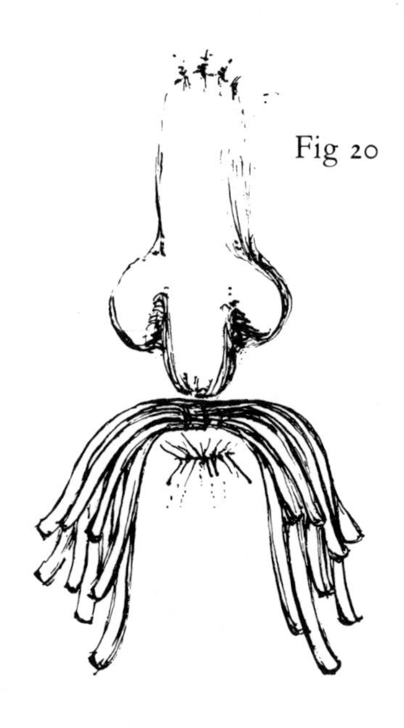
Fig 20

Underbody

Take the body part of the tights and if necessary cut across the crotch to give a tube open at both ends. Gather round the cut edge and sew it to the puppet's neck. Put the head on the forefinger of your right hand and extend your thumb and third finger for the arms. Cut a small hole through the tights at these points.

Hands

(A more simple alternative to those described below are the hands for the Baby in a Bed, p. 55. Use the underbody pattern on p. 55, cutting it off where the hands join the shoulder. Slipstitch these hands to the holes already cut in the underbody.)

Take 2 pipe cleaners and twist the ends together; then take another 2 and do the same. Twist the joined lengths of pipe cleaner together so that you now have a double length. Draw a simple hand on paper to the measurements shown in fig. 22, and bend the pipe cleaners to this shape. Cut 2 lengths of card, each about 2 by 4 in., roll and stick one to a good fit of your thumb and the other to a good fit of your third finger.

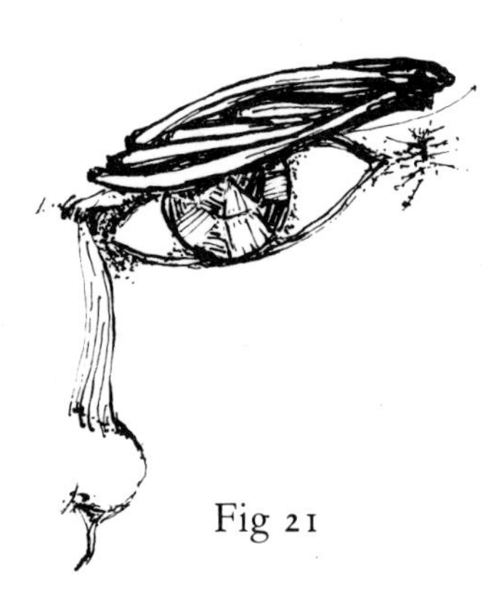
Fig 21

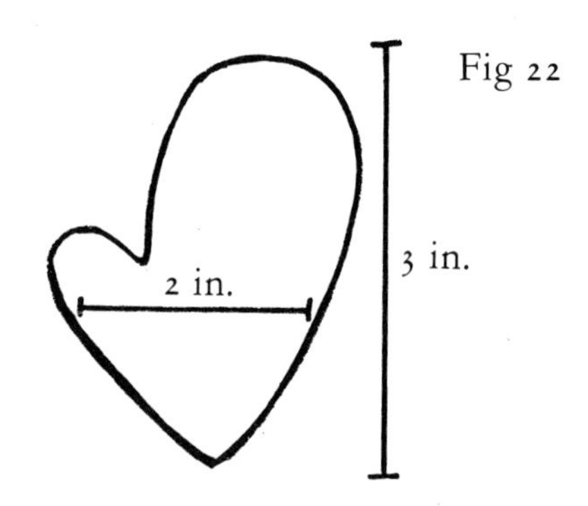

Fig 22

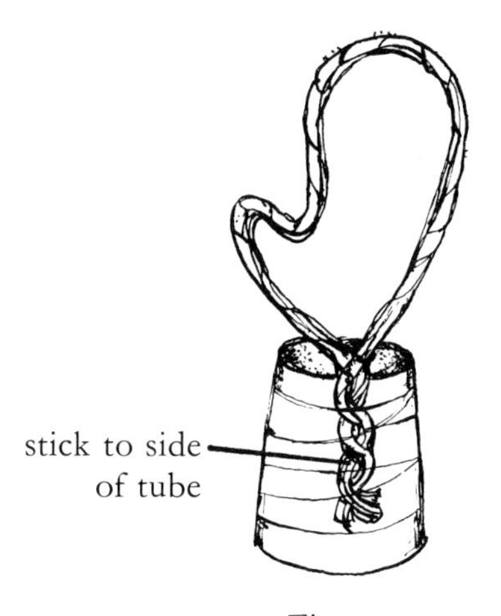

Fig 23

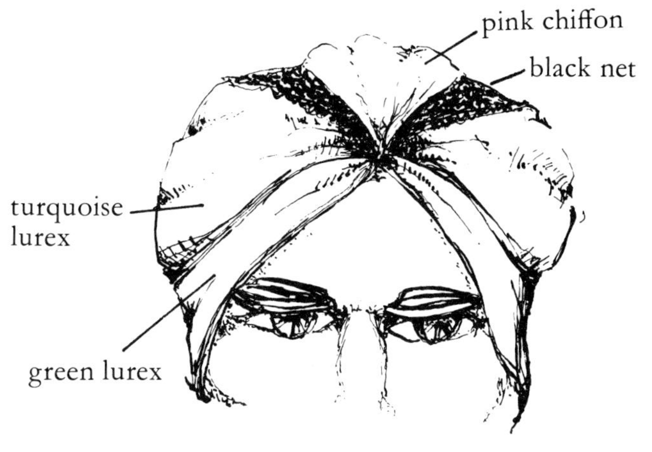

Fig 24

Fasten the pipe cleaner hands to the card tubes by wrapping them with an adhesive strip, as shown in fig. 23.

Cut 2 5-in. lengths of stocking from the ankle ends of the tights. Gather one cut end tightly. Turn the gathering to the inside. Slip the resulting stocking bag over the hand shape and catch the gathered part to the pipe cleaner frame, at the centre of the finger portion. Stuff the hand with kapok, sew divisions for the fingers and thumb and stitch the hand into shape in the same way as you did the face. Take care to make a pair of hands. The pipe cleaners can be bent to make them curve over more realistically. Tie a thread round and round firmly where the wrist would be and leave the rest of the stocking hanging.

Attaching the Hands to the Body

Slip the puppet on your left hand with your thumb and third finger through the holes you have cut; then put the hands in place. Pin the stocking arms to the underbody. Make sure the thumbs of the puppet's hands are uppermost.

Take your hand out and trim away any excess on the arms; then sew them in place.

Clothes

Turban

Cut a length of turquoise blue lurex material about 14 in. by 7 in. Press in the raw edge along one long side. Gather the two shorter ends, arrange and pin the strip of material round the puppet's head, and stitch one end over the other in the centre of the forehead. Gather the remaining long edge and draw it up. Before securing the thread you may need to stuff the turban slightly to give a good full shape. Other strips of material can now be added for a more varied colourful effect. The puppet in the illustration has a narrow strip of green lurex bound round the lower edge of the turban and pieces of black net and pink chiffon run from front to back. Drape and pin the materials, then catch lightly in place.

Add an aigrette of some kind to the forehead stitching of the turban. In the illustration this is made from beads and paillettes threaded on wire, with a centre of an attractive button; but it may consist of feathers, or one or two glass jewels, as you wish.

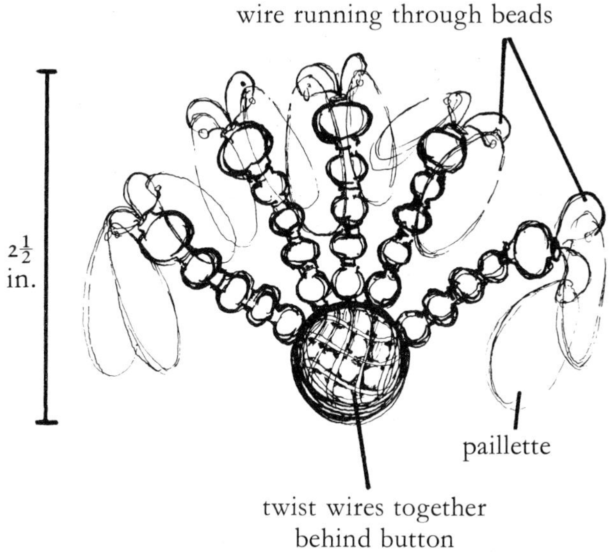

wire running through beads

$2\frac{1}{2}$ in.

paillette

twist wires together
behind button

Fig 25

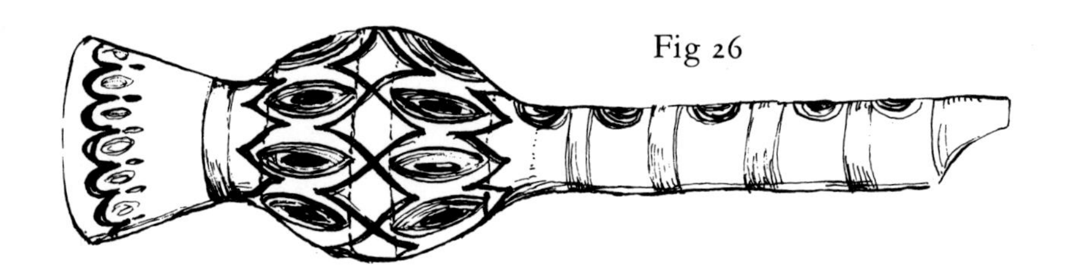
Fig 26

Robe

Sleeves Cut 2 pieces of green lurex, on the bias if possible, each 7 in. by 5½ in., and press in one long edge for ½ in. Join the short edges and run gathering threads along the turned-in edges. Oversew the other long edges to prevent fraying. Slip the sleeves over the arms and draw up the gathering threads to fit the wrists. Catch the other ends in place.

Main part Cut a piece of green lurex 15 by 20 in. Press in ½ in. on both long edges and stitch down one of them. Oversew the short edges to prevent fraying.

Cut a central panel of turquoise lurex 6 by 15 in. Press in ½ in. on the 2 shorter edges and stitch down one of them. Oversew the longer edges.

Now decorate the central panel in any way you wish. The coloured illustration shows a suggestion. First a triple thickness of black net 2½ in. wide by 14 in. long is stitched down the centre. Over this comes a 1¼ in. strip of double pink chiffon, with a length of silver braid along the middle. Pink paillettes are sewn at random over the decoration.

With right sides together, pin the centre panel to the 15 in. edges of the green part of the robe. Stitch them together for 2 in.; leave a gap of 3 in. for the arms, then continue stitching to the lower edge. Run a gathering thread all round the top edge; slip the robe on the puppet and draw up the thread to fit the neck. Stitch the gathering in place and add a length of silver braid to hide the stitching. Catch the arm openings in place round the sleeves.

Pipe

Take the 6 in. length of ½ in. dowel. Make up some wallpaper or flour paste (a solution of flour and water boiled like a white sauce), and wrap torn kitchen towel, soaked in glue, round the wood to the shape shown in fig. 26. Whittle the straight end to a blunted point. The dowel may also be left plain. Paint the pipe with enamel, fit it in the puppet's right hand—the one on the thumb tube—and sew the hand firmly in place.

SNAKE

Materials

1 stocking or leg of tights, in pale colour and a thick weave; 2 ping pong balls; 2 pipe cleaners; snake's scales of approx. 100 large green sequins or paillettes with a hole at the tip and 50 pink ones; or pieces green and pink lurex material to cut into shapes; 7 by 4 in. piece pink velvet or similar for mouth; scrap orange felt; emerald dye; silver foil.

To Make

Dye the stocking emerald green. Cut off the welt, but do not discard it, and oversew the raw edge. If you are using an old pair of tights cut off the body part and use one leg; oversew round the top. Measure 19 in. from the oversewn end and cut the stocking here. This length should be sufficient to enclose the arm and hand from the finger tip to just past the elbow. Adjust the measurement if necessary.

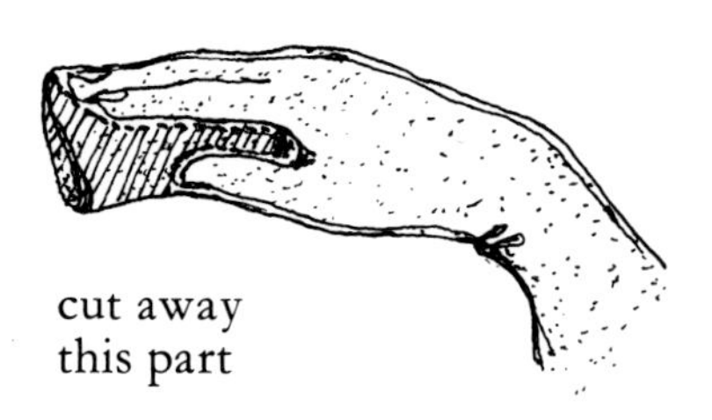

Fig 27

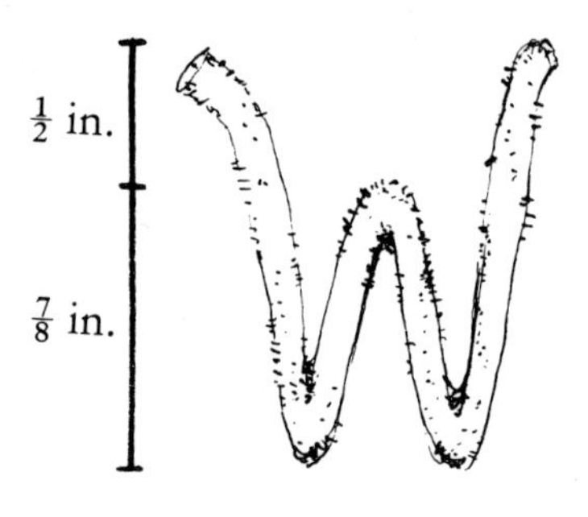

Fig 28

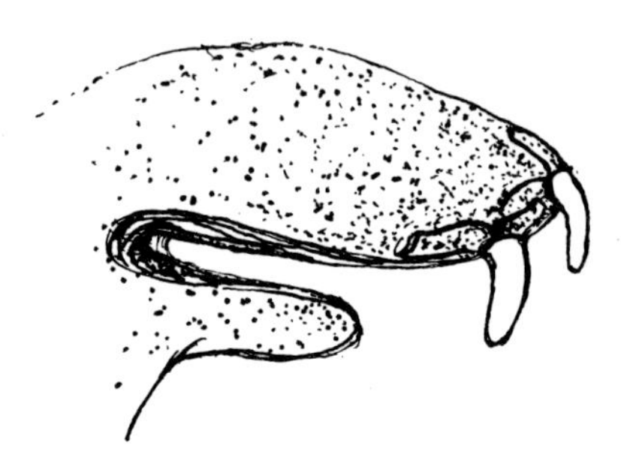

Fig 29

Turn the stocking inside out and pull it over your left hand and arm. Extend your thumb as shown in fig. 27 to shape the snake's lower jaw, and cut away the diagonally shaded part of the stocking on both sides of your hand. Fold the pink material in half across the width and fit it into the join of the thumb to the hand, with the right side of the material next to the fingers. Pin it to the cut edge of the stocking. Slip off the stocking and trim the pink material to shape, then oversew the two raw edges together.

Fangs

For each fang bend a pipe cleaner into the shape shown in fig. 28. Cut off excess. Press the folds together and smear them with adhesive, then wind foil around leaving the two ½ in. lengths of pipe cleaner uncovered. Stick the ends of the foil.

With the scissors tip make 2 small holes in the stocking about ½ in. apart at the point of the upper jaw, then press the uncovered ends of the fangs through the holes. Open out these short pieces of pipe cleaner to stop the fangs slipping out of place, and add a few stitches through the stocking to secure them.

Fig 30

Tongue

Cut a piece of orange felt as shown in fig. 31, and stick it to the centre of the lower jaw.

Scales

Sew the sequins or paillettes loosely all over the top of the snake, starting at the fang end of the upper jaw. Leave the under side plain. Failing sequins, cut ovals each about 1 in. long by ¾ in. wide from lurex material and sew them by one end to the stocking. Don't worry if the material frays as the loose threads will give a more blurred, impressionistic appearance to the snake. You may find it simpler to slip the stocking over a rolling pin as you sew on the scales, to make the puppet more easily handled.

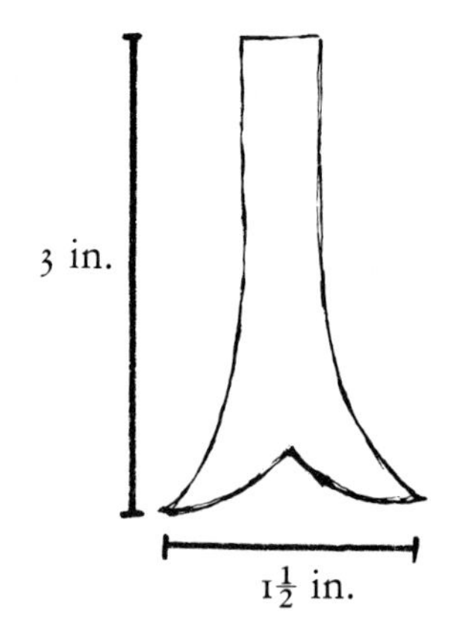

Fig 31

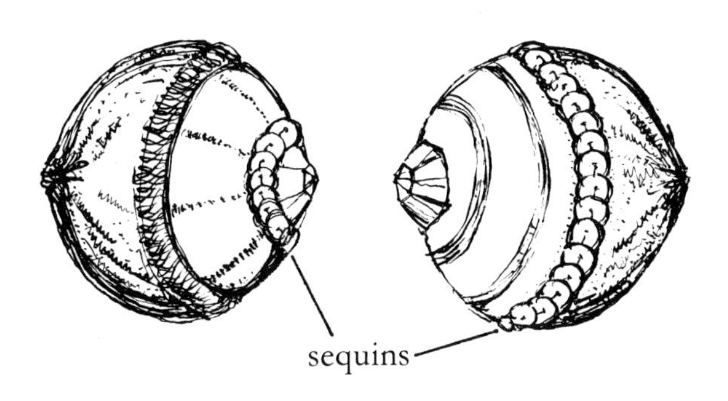

Fig 32

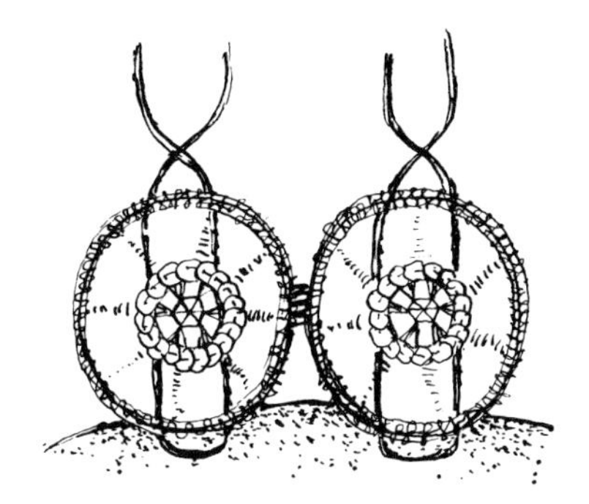

Fig 33

Eyes
Spray the ping pong balls silver and then paint them with pearly pink nail polish or colour with a felt tip pen. Alternatively you can paint them any light shade which will tone in with the snake's colour scheme.

From the welt of the stocking cut a piece about 5 by $1\frac{1}{2}$ in. Oversew the short edges together and gather along one long raw edge; turn to right side. Fit this little cap over half a painted ping pong ball to represent an eyelid. Glue a green glass 'jewel' in the centre of the uncovered portion for the pupil, then decorate the rest of the eye with other sequins or lurex braiding, or paint rings of various colours on it. Suggestions are given in fig. 32.

Place the eyes side by side as shown in fig. 33, and catch the eyelids. together. Thread a long darning needle with strong cotton and push the needle right through one of the ping pong balls from the top to the opposite side; stitch through the stocking at the point where the eye is to be situated and come up again through the ball. Tie the threads together at the top. See figs. 33 and 34, for the approximate position of the eyes and their attachment.

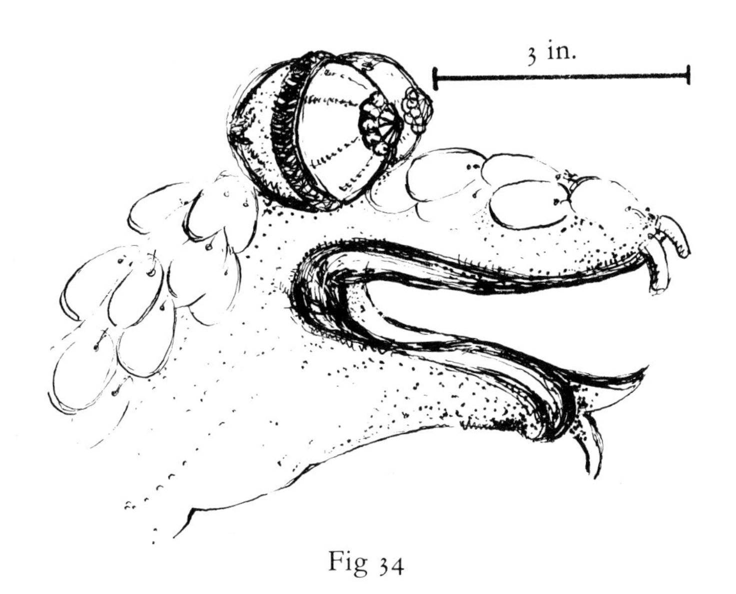

Fig 34

Dragon

This dragon can be the nucleus of many a puppet play. There are many possibilities for its decoration. Sequins in any suitable colour and small or large glass 'jewels' may be quickly stuck in place rather than sewn, using any clear adhesive. An interesting patchy shaded effect is rapidly given by short bursts of gold spray paint on the appropriate green satin parts, after they are made up. Shield any parts not to be painted with paper. If you are really clever a pièce de resistance would be to have a baleful light shining forth from inside the dragon's mouth, by means of a tiny bulb wired to a torch battery which is held in a pocket inside the dragon's body.

Materials
For jaw: 12 by 5 in. piece thick card; 15 by 8 in. piece thin red material; cotton wool to pad.
For tongue: 3 by 5 in. red material; stuffing.
For teeth: 14 by 4 in. silver material; thin card.
For spine strip: 4 by 16 in. red felt; thin card.
For top body and scale strips: $\frac{1}{2}$ yd. green satin.
For eyes: 2 1-inch. diameter buttons.
For underbody: $\frac{1}{4}$ yd. material.
For wings: $2\frac{1}{4}$ yds. stout wire; 6 by 10 in. transparent material.
Iron-on adhesive stiffening for green satin and underbody material.
Sequins and other decorations.
Scraps of foam rubber to stuff.

To Make
Jaw
Cut paper patterns from the squared diagram on p. 28.

From thick card cut an identical upper and lower jaw. Spread one side of each piece of card with adhesive and press on a thin even layer of wadding or cotton wool.

Take a piece of thin red material 8 by 15 in.—rayon taffeta, fine wool or metallic material are all suitable—and fold in half across the width. Put the straight edge of the paper pattern to the fold and cut the material with a surplus of $1\frac{1}{2}$ in. all round the curved edges.

Open out the fabric and lay the card pieces wadding side down on it with their straight edges touching. Apply adhesive to the surplus material, fold it

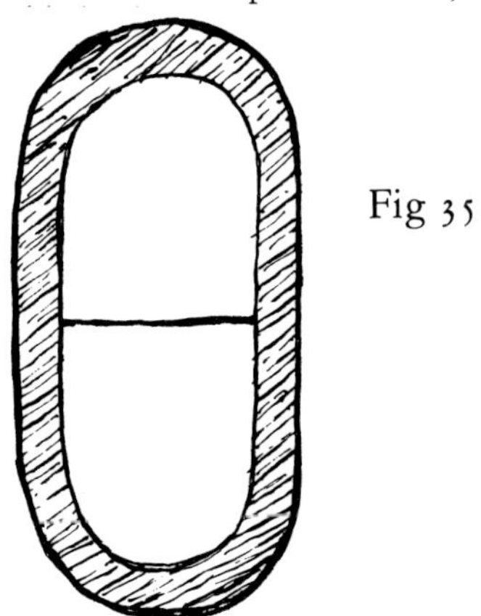

Fig 35

over to the unpadded side of the card and stick down well.

Tongue
Cut a pattern for the tongue from the squared diagram, and an identical back and front from red, orange or emerald green material. Seam allowance has already been given. Pin the two pieces together, wrong sides facing, and machine or back stitch $\frac{1}{2}$ in. away from each slanted edge. Turn to right side and stuff the tongue lightly.

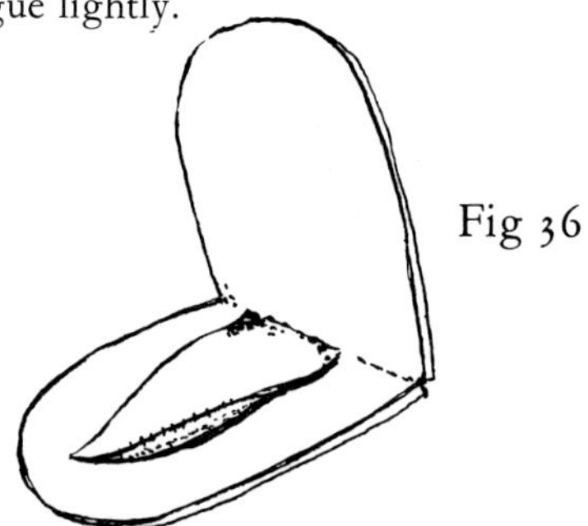

Fig 36

Fold the top edges $\frac{1}{2}$ in. to the inside and slip stitch together; then stick the tongue to one of the padded sides of the jaw, with the straight edge touching the hinge of material between the two halves.

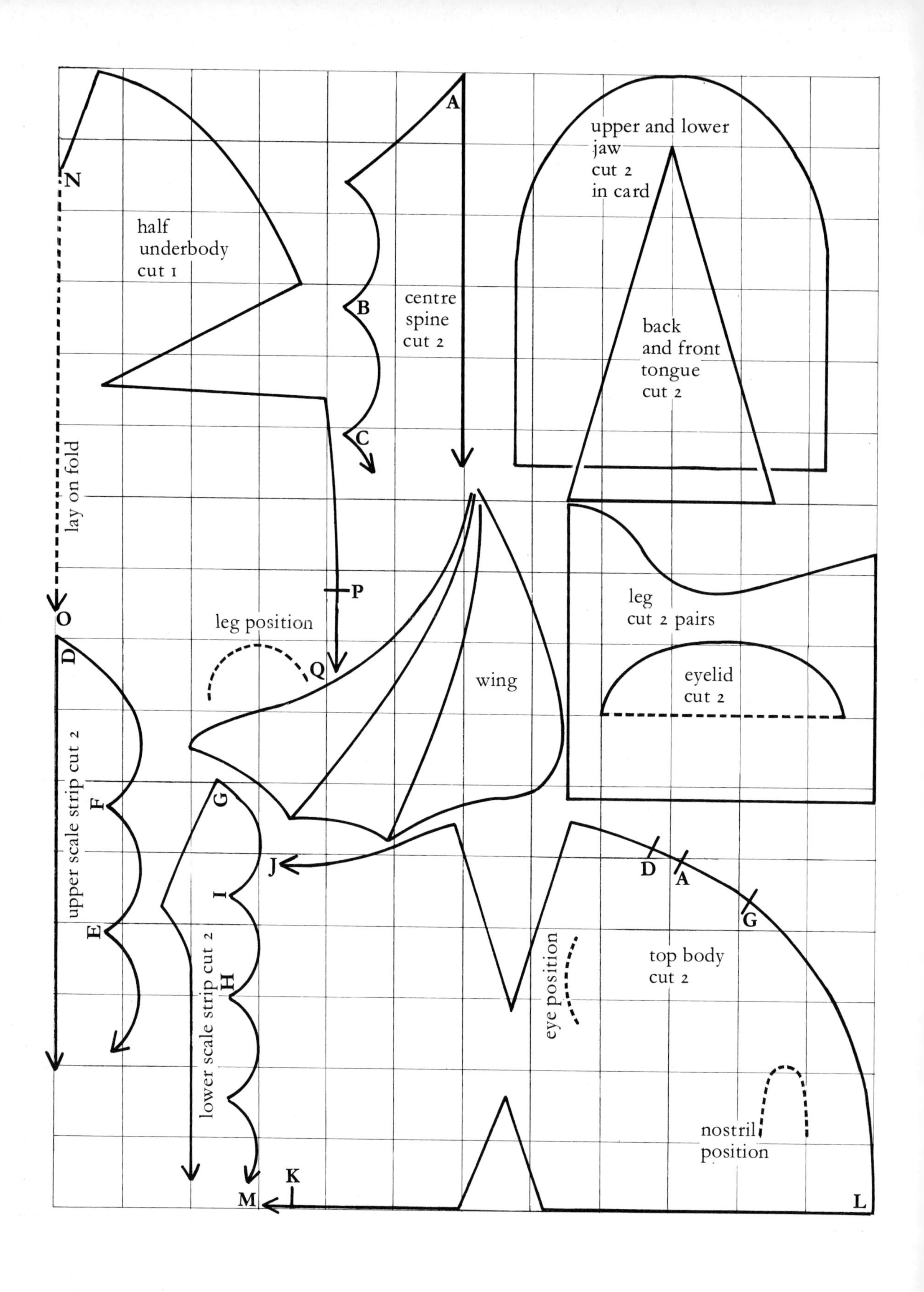

half
underbody
cut 1
N
lay on fold
O
A
B
C
centre
spine
cut 2
upper and lower
jaw
cut 2
in card
back
and front
tongue
cut 2
P
Q
leg position
wing
leg
cut 2 pairs
eyelid
cut 2
D
upper scale strip cut 2
F
E
G
I
H
lower scale strip cut 2
J
D
A
G
top body
cut 2
eye position
nostril
position
K
M
L

Teeth
Cut 2 strips of thin card, each 14 in. long by $\frac{1}{2}$ in. wide.

Cut 2 pieces of silver material each 14 in. long by $1\frac{3}{4}$ in. wide.

Fold them in half along the length and lay a strip of card inside each piece. You may need to run a little adhesive along the edges of the material to stop them fraying. Tack each strip together to enclose the card.

Curve a strip along one of the covered halves of the jaw and hold it in place temporarily by pins placed at right angles to the card. The strip should be allowed to taper into each corner of the jaw, so that when the mouth is closed the teeth will not be in the way.

With a strong needle and double thread oversew the teeth strip to the curved jaw edges, beginning at the corner. Push the needle up through the covered jaw edge and through the teeth strip simultaneously; continue to sew firmly all round. Fasten the other strip in place by the same method. The stitches will eventually be covered so it does not matter if they are untidy.

To mark the division of the teeth, thread thick soft embroidery cotton into a darning needle and take large oversewing stitches, 2 or 3 in the same place, at $\frac{1}{2}$ in. intervals all round each strip. See fig. 38.

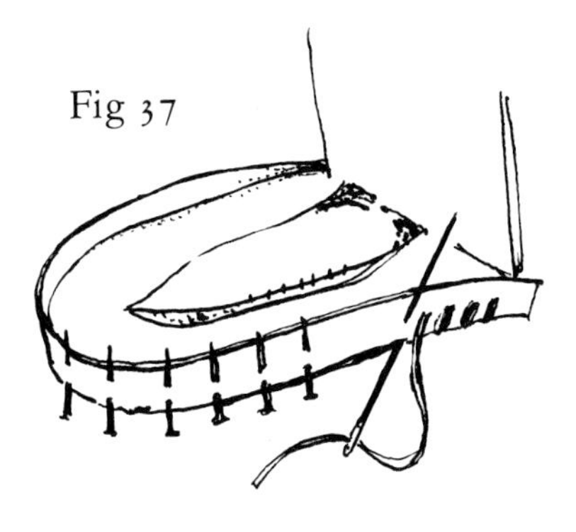

Fig 37

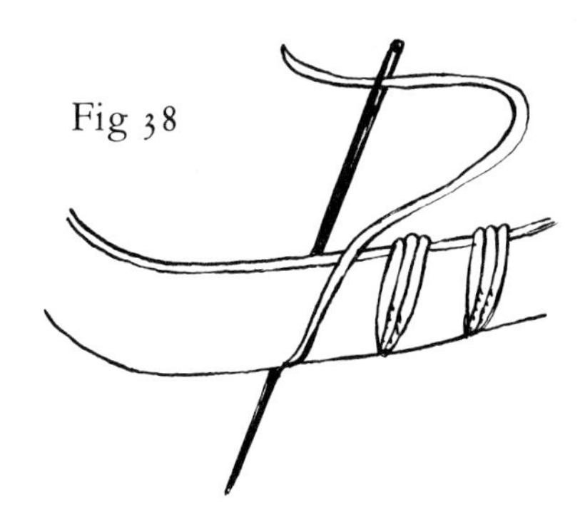

Fig 38

Body

Centre Spine Part of the pattern for the centre spine is given in the squared diagram on p. 28. A indicates the forehead end of the spine. The scallop B to C should be repeated until the strip is $15\frac{1}{2}$ in. long.

Cut 2 identical spine strips from red felt. Cut an inner layer to the same pattern from thin card but subtract $\frac{1}{2}$ in. from the width. Oversew the felt strips neatly together along the scalloped edges, slip the card in between them and sew a line of running stitches just below its straight edge.

Scale Strips Part of the pattern for the upper and lower scale strips is given in the squared diagram on p. 28.

On the upper scale strip, D indicates the forehead end. Repeat the scallop E to F until the pattern measures $14\frac{1}{2}$ in. along the lower edge.

On the lower scale strip, G indicates the forehead end.

Repeat the scallop H to I until the pattern measures $16\frac{1}{2}$ in. along the lower edge.

Cut 2 upper and 2 lower scale strips from green satin, and iron the wrong side of each one on to adhesive stiffening. Add any decoration to them at this point.

Top Body Cut a paper pattern for half the top body following the squared diagram on p. 28.

Fig 39

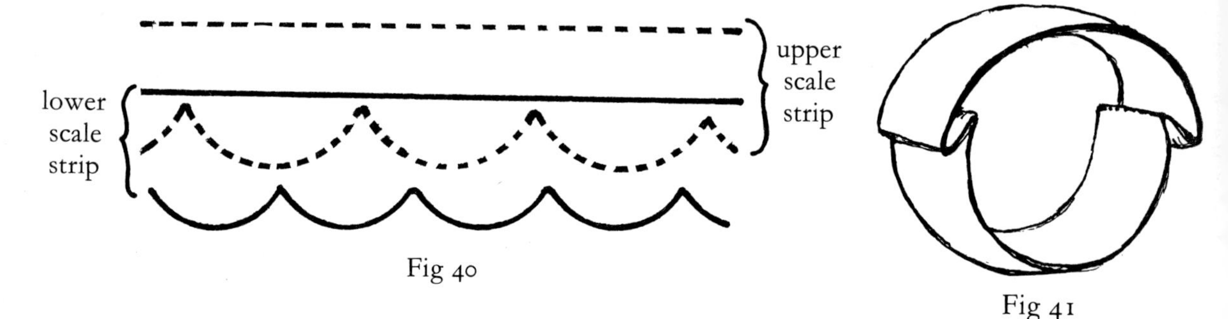

Fig 40

Fig 41

The arrows on the pattern indicate that these lines should be drawn out until L to M measures $17\frac{1}{2}$ in. including the lower dart.

Fold the piece of green satin for the body in half lengthways, with wrong sides together, and pin the pattern on to the double material. Cut out 2 half top bodies. Iron the wrong sides of each on to adhesive stiffening. Mark points D, A, G and K with tacking stitches. Mark the nostril and eye positions with tailor's tacks. Oversew the darts together.

Now tack the straight edge of an upper scale strip to the upper edge of each body half, placing the end of each strip D to the point D on the body.

The straight edge of each lower scale strip should be concealed by the scallops of the upper one. In fig. 40 the upper strip is therefore indicated by dotted lines. Place the end G of each strip to the point G on the pattern and tack the rest in place to each body half. Oversew firmly. Small pleats may be made to ease in excess at the forehead end of the body.

Finally, the centre spine must be tacked in place before the two halves of the body can be joined together.

Place the end of the spine strip A to the point marked A on one of the body halves. Pin the straight edge to the straight edge of the top body. The upper scale strip will be sandwiched in between the top body and the spine. Tack all layers together along the edges.

Now place the right sides of each body half together and tack from the lower point of the curve L right round to J. Machine or back stitch $\frac{1}{2}$ in. away from the edge, enclosing the spine and the two upper scale strips as you sew.

Oversew the straight edges J to M on each half to neaten them. Decorate the body if you wish.

Eyes

Choose 2 large flat buttons, each 1 in. in diameter. The ones on the dragon illustrated were white with a silver centre. A large red 'jewel' has been glued off-centre to each for a pupil.

For the surround of each eye, cut a piece of gold metallic material $2\frac{1}{2}$ in. by 5 in. Catch the short ends together and fold the strip in half lengthways. Make 2 pleats in the resulting tube as shown in fig. 41, flatten one end and catch it together, and sew this new

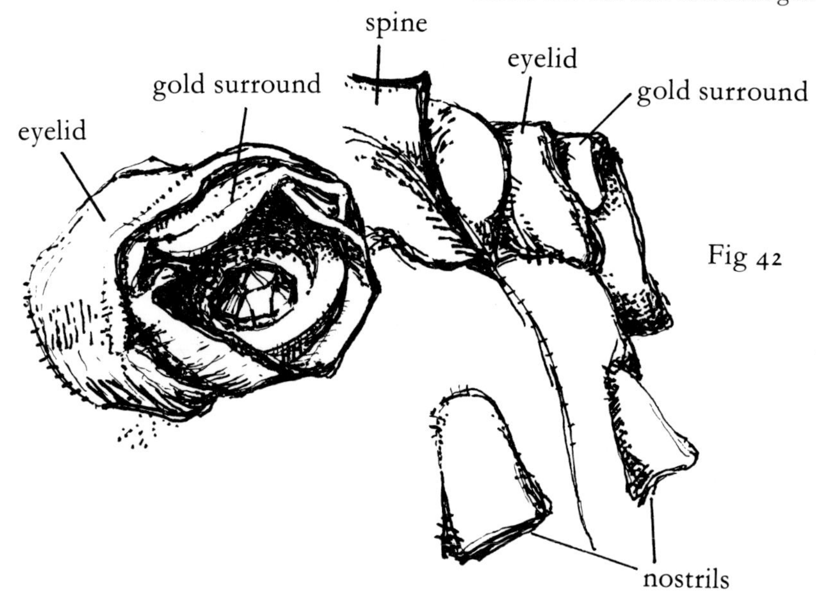

Fig 42

flat part to the place shown by the dotted lines in the diagram.

Stick the under part of the tube to the green satin.

Push a button eye well inside the tube and sew or stick down, so that the button lies flat against the lower part of the gold surround.

Cut the paper pattern for the eyelid from the squared diagram on p. 28, and lay the dotted line against the doubled edge of a piece of green satin 4 by $2\frac{1}{2}$ in. folded lengthways. Cut round the curved edge; surplus for turn-in is already given. Press a $\frac{1}{4}$ in. to one side of the doubled material all round the curved edge, and stick or sew the eyelid all round the top of the gold eye surround to the green satin body. Pleats and gathers are all permissible to make it fit, and if it's lumpy it will all add to the aged warty effect!

Make the other eye in the same way. A view of the complete assembly is shown in fig. 42.

Nostrils

For one nostril cut a piece of red felt 4 in. by 1 in. and roll it up widthways to give a tube 1 in. by about $\frac{3}{4}$ in. wide. Flatten one end of the tube and catch it together. Sew and stick it to the snout at the dotted lines shown on the diagram. Make the other nostril in the same way.

Wings

The pattern for the wings is given in the squared diagram on p. 28

Draw a paper pattern first, marking in the ribs. Cut 3 lengths of pliable stout wire for each wing, 23 in., 8 in. and 9 in. The 23 in. length will make the outline of the wing, the 8 and 9 in. lengths the inner strengthening ribs. With pliers wind an inch of the 8 in. length round the 23 in. length of wire, 9 in. away from one of its ends. Do the same with one inch of the 9 in. length, this time $10\frac{1}{2}$ in. away from the same end. See fig. 43. These short lengths may be fastened firmly into place by winding finer wire round the joins, or by binding with adhesive tape, the kind used for dressing injuries, or the electrical insulating variety. Do not worry if the result is lumpy.

Now wrap all the wire with emerald green or red bias binding, in the same way as a lampshade is wrapped (fig. 44). Start and finish 3 in. from each end of the 23 in. length of wire. Leave the last 3 in. of each shorter wire also unwrapped.

Lay the wire on the paper pattern and see that the shorter lengths of wire coincide with the ribs you have marked in. Bend the 23 in. length round the outline of the wing; note that the unwrapped portions of each wire should project below the lowest point of the wing.

Twist all 4 unwrapped pieces of wire together and cover them with bias binding, to make an extension.

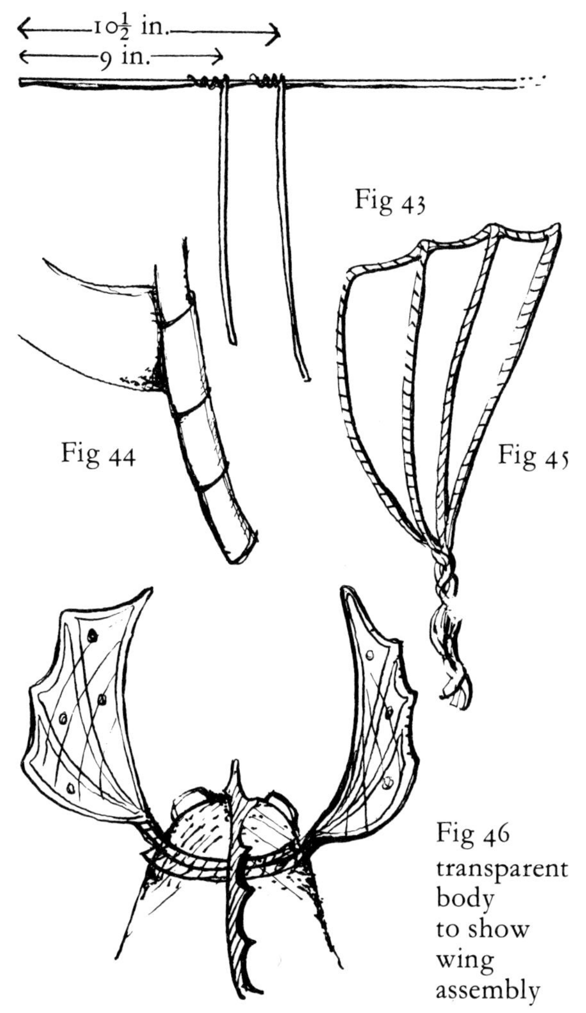

Fig 43

Fig 44

Fig 45

Fig 46 transparent body to show wing assembly

To make the wing covering, cut a piece of any suitable transparent material $\frac{1}{2}$ in. larger all round than the paper pattern, turn in $\frac{1}{2}$ in. on the edges and pin them to the covered wire shape with the pins at right angles to the wire. Sew the material to the tape.

Make another wing the same, and decorate them.

To attach the wings to the body, pierce holes with the point of the scissors through each top body half just under the scalloped edge of the lower scale strips. The exact placing of these holes does not matter provided they match on both sides. The dragon illustrated was pierced 6 in. away from point H, measuring in a straight line. Bend the 3 in. extensions at right angles to each wing and push them through the holes. Sew the ends of the extensions together as much as possible, and stitch them to the top of the dragon. In fig. 46 the assembly of the wings to the dragon's body is drawn, but the scale strips are not shown, for the sake of clarity.

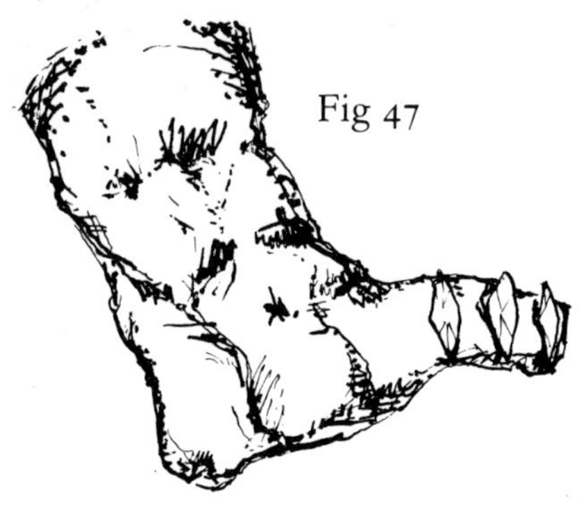
Fig 47

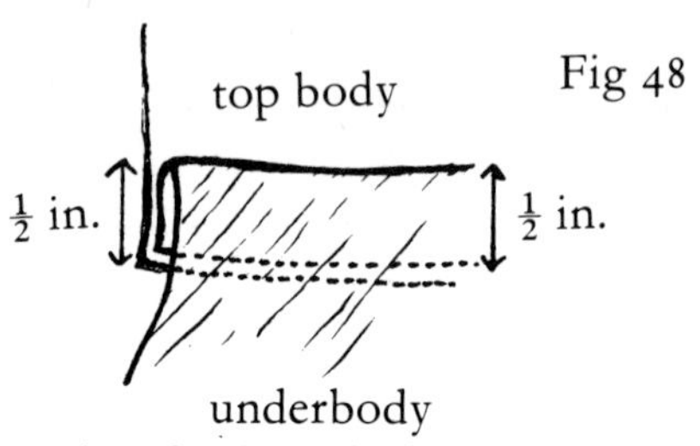

Fig 48

Underbody
The pattern for half the underbody is given in the diagram on p. 28. Draw out the arrowed lines until N to O measures 16½ in.

The underbody is cut all in one piece. Fold the material in half lengthways and lay the dotted line N to O against the fold. Iron the wrong side of the material on to adhesive stiffening; mark point P and the leg positions, shown by the dotted lines, by tailor's tacks. Oversew the darts and neaten the straight end O to Q by oversewing.

Legs
Cut a pattern for the legs from the squared diagram on p. 28. Cut 2 pairs of green satin legs, remembering to reverse the pattern for the second half of each pair. Place the pairs together, wrong sides facing, and with ½ in. seam machine or backstitch together, leaving the tops open. Turn to right side and stuff firmly. Turn ½ in. in at the tops and ladderstitch the legs firmly to the underbody, keeping the top open in a round shape.

To make the legs appear wrinkled and less like little boots, pucker the material by running short gathering threads through for an inch or so at irregular intervals; and stab stitch right through the legs from side to side to give deep clefts. Claws may be indicated by long stitches in gold, or by gold oval sequins.

To Join the Top Body to the Underbody
Press ½ in. to the wrong side all round the sides and the curved portion of the underbody.

The folded edge of the underbody should now be pinned ½ in. up from the raw edge of the top body. Place point P to point K of the top body on either side. Oversew the underbody in place from P to Q on either side. The front unsewn portion will contain the jaw.

To Complete
The covered jaw and teeth section is now fastened in place. Press in ½ in. round the jaw line K to L to K on the top body. Position the upper jaw and pin the top body to it, with pins placed at right angles to the teeth. The green satin should just cover the previous stitches. With double thread oversew the body firmly to the teeth. Attach the underbody in the same way. The forehead and underjaw need stuffing slightly to make them appear more solid. Apply adhesive to scrap lengths of foam rubber and press these to the inside of the top and bottom jaw, experimenting from time to time to make sure your hand still fits comfortably in place. Failing foam rubber, rolled up lengths of newspaper can be used.

Fig 49
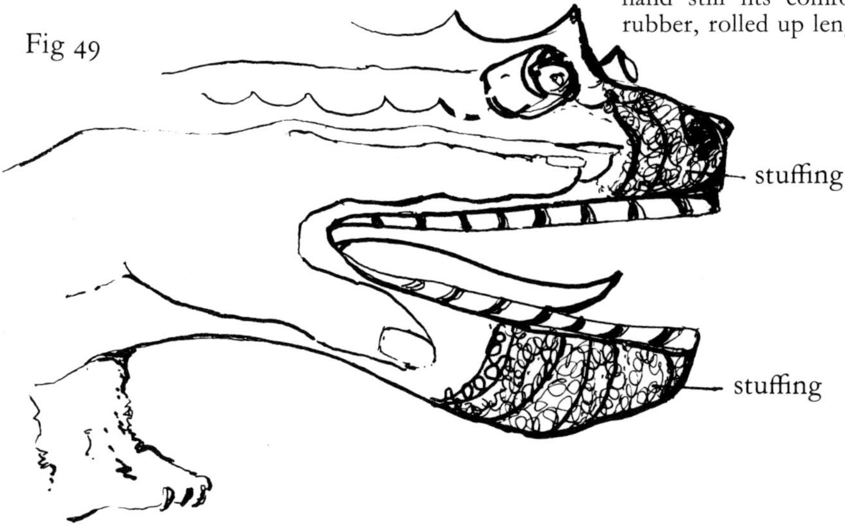

Part Two
Puppets with Moving Legs

This type of puppet is a small doll with pockets for the first and second fingers at the back of its legs. A loop of elastic holds the body firmly to the manipulator's hands.

Dutch Dolls

The dutch dolls can dance with tapping sabots, thanks to the thimbles inside the bottom of their legs.

After making them you may like to experiment with a family of dolls to act stories you have invented. Make the mother and father the same size and shape as the dutch dolls, but without the hats on their heads. Give the mother an apron and omit the corselet belt. Make her legs brown to resemble stockings. The sabots can have the upturned points tucked in to appear more like shoes. For the father, elongate the jacket and make the legs the same colour as the jacket, to look like ordinary trousers. Give him a white collar and tie, and perhaps a bowler hat. Various children can have smaller top bodies and shorter legs, though the width of the pocket for the legs will have to remain the same to fit the fingers manipulating them. Finally, the mother can hold in her arms a baby wrapped in a shawl: clasp him firmly to her bosom by means of a press stud shared between them.

Materials

Sufficient to make both:—
1 9-in. square of pink felt; 1 9-in. square of yellow felt.
For each puppet:—
2 lead dress weights each about $\frac{3}{4}$ in. diameter; 5 in. round elastic; 2 3-in. lengths cord or string; 2 thimbles; piece card 5 by 3 in.
In addition for Boy:—
Black felt 6 by $4\frac{1}{2}$ in.; red felt 3 by 4 in.; scraps of turquoise and white felt; 2 tiny gold beads or gold sequins.
In addition for Girl:—
White felt 8 by 7 in.; turquoise felt 8 by $4\frac{1}{2}$ in.; scraps of black and pink felt; 9 in. of narrow broderie anglaise or lace; 6 in. narrow ribbon or gold trimming.

To Make Both Puppets

Redraw the patterns from the squared diagram on p. 39 and trace the actual size patterns.

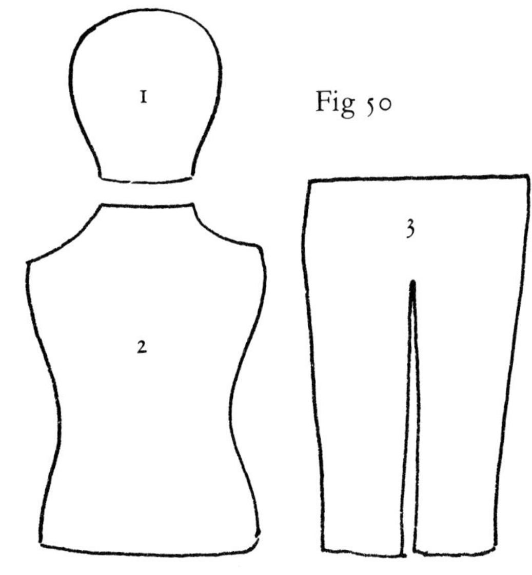

Fig 50

C

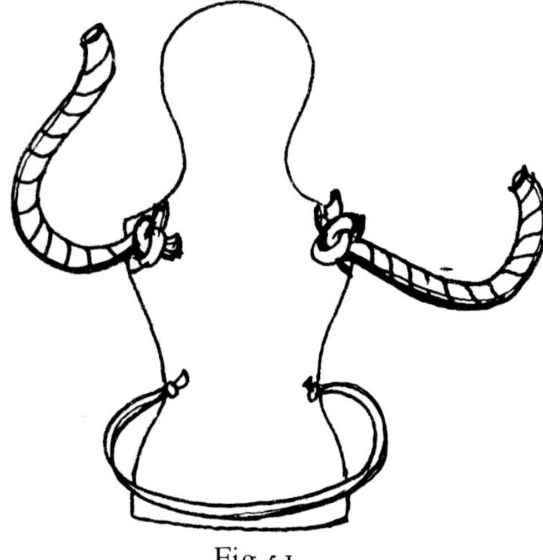

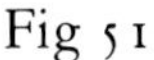

Fig 51

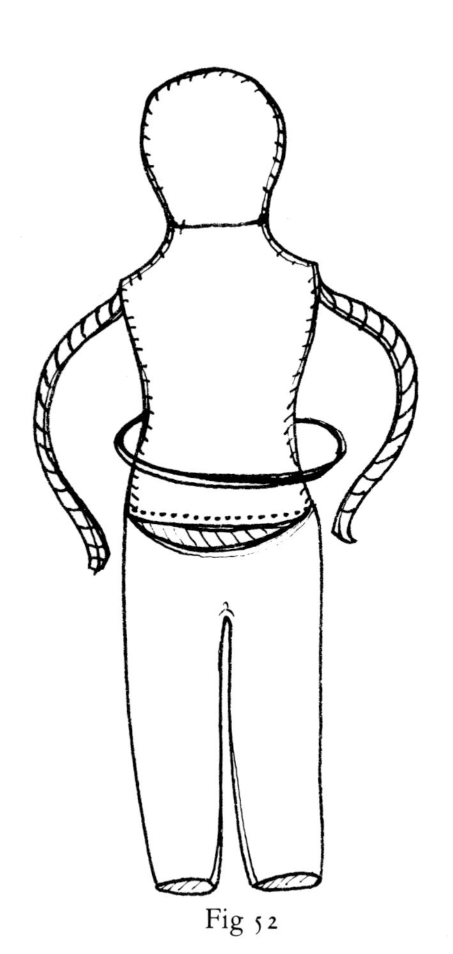

Fig 52

The Card Stiffening

Fold the body pattern along the dotted line B-E, so that the legs are out of sight, and draw round the upper portion only on some fairly stout card, such as that used in a shoebox. This shape is the torso stiffening. Cut the card $\frac{1}{8}$ inch inside the outline all round.

The Felt Body

Unfold the paper pattern and cut one complete body in pink felt for the front of each puppet.

Now cut the paper pattern on the dotted lines B-E and C-D. You will have 3 separate pieces, head (1), body back (2) and legs back (3). For the Boy cut piece 1 in pink felt and pieces 2 and 3 in black felt. For the Girl cut pieces 1 and 3 in pink felt and piece 2 in turquoise felt.

Arms and Manipulator's Hand Loop

Take the cord for the arms and tie a knot at one end of each piece. With 2 or 3 stitches oversew a knot to the shoulder of each card, to hold the cords lightly in place until they are finally secured. Trim each so that $2\frac{3}{4}$ in. is hanging.

Knot the length of elastic at each end and in the same way attach the knots to either side of the card at the waist.

With the elastic loop at the back smear adhesive all over one side of the card and stick down a thin padding of cotton wool.

The Body Sewing

First, form the pocket for the fingers which move the puppet's legs. Pin the pink felt body front to the piece for the legs back and oversew from A to B and from E to F along the outside of each leg. Leave the ankle edges open, then sew from G up to H, putting a few extra stitches in at this point, and down again to I. Turn the part you have just sewn inside out.

Now place the padded side of the card torso stiffening to the wrong side of the pink body front. Slip the body back of the puppet under the elastic loop, and with the card sandwiched in between the felt layers pin the body back to the body front. You may find it easier to stick the back to the card to hold it in place as well as using a few pins. Let the cord for the arms hang free. Oversew neatly all round the side and shoulder edges, from B to C and from D to E, taking 2 or 3 extra stitches through the elastic loop ends and the arm cords as you pass to make sure they are firmly fastened in place. Sew the front and back bodies together with a line of stab stitch from E to B, thus enclosing the card lower edge.

Pin the back of the head to the front and oversew them together. Catch the back of the head to the back of the body along the neck line C-D.

The back of the puppet should now look like fig. 52.

The Feet
Because the first finger is shorter than the second, the inside of one thimble needs to be padded at the bottom. Stick scraps of felt in place with adhesive until there is sufficient to equalize the length of the fingers when the thimbles are worn by the manipulator.

Smear adhesive lightly round the outer sides of each thimble and push them down inside the legs of each puppet until their tips protrude slightly from the ankle openings. If the felt fits loosely round the thimbles bind a thread round a few times to gather it in slightly.

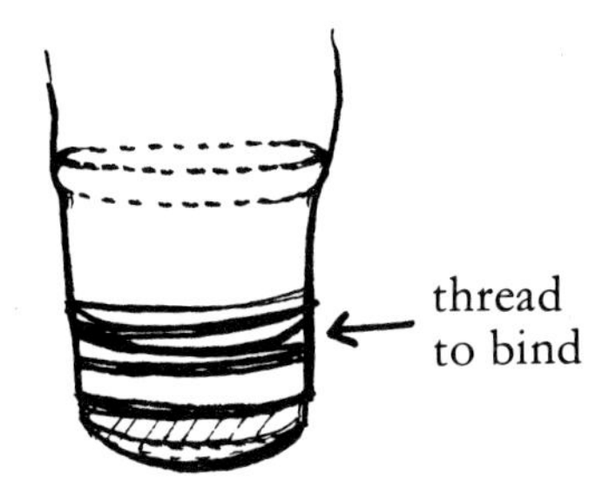

Fig 53

For the Girl, cut 2 pieces of felt $\frac{3}{4}$ in. wide and long enough to wrap round each ankle. These will suggest short socks. Stick them lightly in place so that there will be a seam up the centre back, trim surplus and oversew the short ends together.

Cut 2 pieces of yellow felt for each sabot. Oversew them together on the right side from J to K. Stuff this portion firmly with cotton wool and then wrap the remainder round an ankle enclosing a thimble, making sure the tip of the thimble still shows. Trim any surplus and oversew the centre back seam. Catch in place the lower edges, where the heel would be, round the thimble.

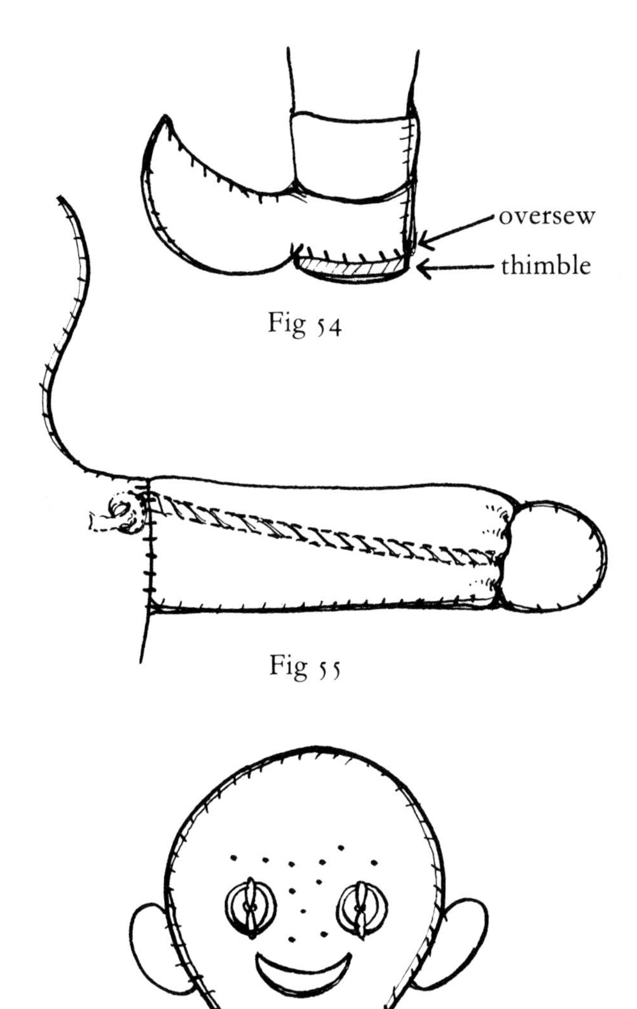

Fig 54

Fig 55

Fig 56

Hands
Cut 4 hand pieces for each puppet. Oversew 2 pieces together for each hand leaving the straight edge open. Cut each dress weight into 2 or 3 pieces with scissors and put one cut-up weight into each hand. Push the cut ends of the arm cord inside the hand so that the uncovered cord will now measure $2\frac{1}{4}$ in. and close the opening, firmly stitching the cord in place.

Sleeves
For each sleeve cut a piece of felt 2 by $2\frac{1}{2}$ in. in white for the Girl and in red for the Boy. Oversew together the long sides of each sleeve and turn the seam to the inside. With the seam at the underarm pull the sleeve over the cord arm and the hand and sew one end to the body and the other to the hand, gathering slightly round the hand as you sew.

To Finish the Boy
Features
Cut 2 blue circles of felt for eyes just over $\frac{1}{4}$ in. diameter and stick these to the face 1 in. from the top of the head and $\frac{1}{2}$ in. apart. If you have 2 small blue sequins sew one to each eye with straight stitches in white cotton; otherwise take one or two straight stitches vertically across the eye. Start and finish the cotton at the back of the head, stitching right through the card and layers of felt to sink the eye slightly. Stick on a curved mouth $\frac{3}{4}$ in. long and $\frac{1}{8}$ in. wide;

Hoppy Rabbit

This simple puppet also has moving legs. If the fur fabric used for making him tends to fray badly allow an extra $\frac{1}{4}$ in. on all edges of the legs pocket so that a slightly larger seam may be taken. Other animals can be created, following the same idea of a little flat fronted head with forelegs sewn behind it—a lion (see the talking lion in part one for ideas about the face)—a kitten, or a puppy with floppy ears are all possibilities.

Fig 61 Fig 62

Materials
10 by 8 in. short pile fur fabric; scraps of card, pink satin; pink, black and white felt; 2 pipe cleaners.

To Make
The legs of the rabbit are cut from the same pattern as the legs of the dutch dolls. Use the squared diagram on p. 39, but draw the leg pieces from below the dotted linc E to B only. Squared diagrams for the face and ears and actual size patterns for the eyes, pupils and eye backings are also given with the dutch doll patterns. Cut 2 leg pieces, 2 faces, 2 ears in fur fabric with the pile running downwards, and 2 ear linings in pink satin, on the bias if possible.

Legs
With right sides facing oversew the raw edges together from B to A, along the lower straight edge A to G, and up to H. Continue in this way around the legs. Machine stitch all round within $\frac{1}{8}$ in. from the edge. Failing a machine, use fine back stitching. Turn work to right side; oversew round the top edge to prevent fraying.

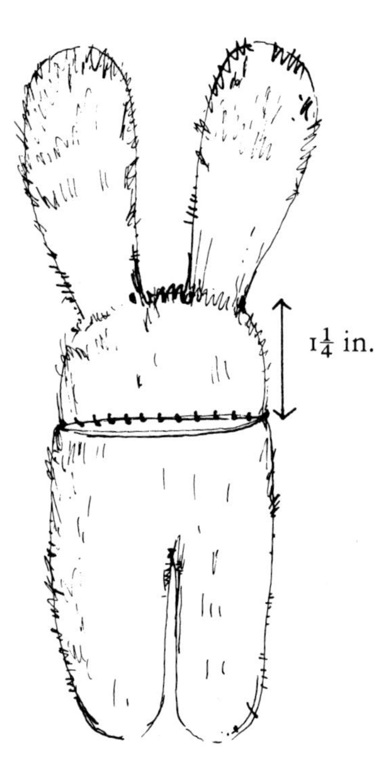

Fig 63

Head
With right sides facing oversew and back stitch round the head from J to K. Turn to right side. Cut a piece of card to the same pattern as the head but $\frac{1}{8}$ in. smaller all round and slip it into the fabric head. Push in kapok or other stuffing to pad one side of the head lightly. Close the gap at the top.

Features
Cut 2 black eye backings, 2 white eyes and 2 pink pupils from felt. Stick them together and sew 2 or 3 small white stitches for highlights in the pink pupils.

$\frac{3}{4}$ in

From
round t
pong b
finish o

Features
For the
it with a
the ends
and sew
push it
the thre
beads fo
See figs.

Wings
Trace th
in card.

Stitch to the face, stabbing right through the card to the back of the head to sink the eyes a little, and following fig. 61. The nose is a small triangle of card, $\frac{1}{2}$ in. along each side, covered with a bias scrap of pink satin whose raw edges are caught together at the back; or use a triangle of pink felt. For the mouth cut 2 strips of pink felt, $\frac{3}{8}$ in. and $1\frac{1}{4}$ in. long by $\frac{1}{8}$ in. wide. Catch the shorter length vertically under the nose and curve the other strip under it. Take three white stitches for whiskers on either side of the face.

Ears
With right sides together place the ear linings to the ears, oversew and machine or back stitch together around the curved upper edges. Leave the straight lower edges open. Turn work to the right side. Bend each pipe cleaner in a curve following the arch of the ear and slip one inside each. Fold the ear bases in half and stitch to the head; see coloured illustration.

To Complete
Sew an upper edge of the leg pocket to the back of the rabbit's head, $1\frac{1}{4}$ in. below the upper curve.

Kangaroo and Baby

This toy is actually two puppets combined, the mother operated by the hand and the baby by a rod. In conversation between the two there are many possibilities for back chat from baby and scoldings from Mum, or loving affection.

Materials
$\frac{1}{4}$ yd. light brown fleecy material such as acrilan, velvet or short pile fur fabric: alternatively felt could be used; $\frac{1}{4}$ yd. apricot fleecy material; scraps apricot, mid and dark brown felt; pair large brown glass eyes; pair small black or brown beads; kapok to stuff; $\frac{1}{4}$ yd. round elastic; 6 by 2 in. piece thin card; pipe cleaners or wire to stiffen tail; 9 in. length of dowel about $\frac{3}{8}$ in. thick.

To Make Mother
Cut patterns for legs, head and ears from the squared diagram below. The patterns for the paws, tail, front and side bodies are on p. 47.

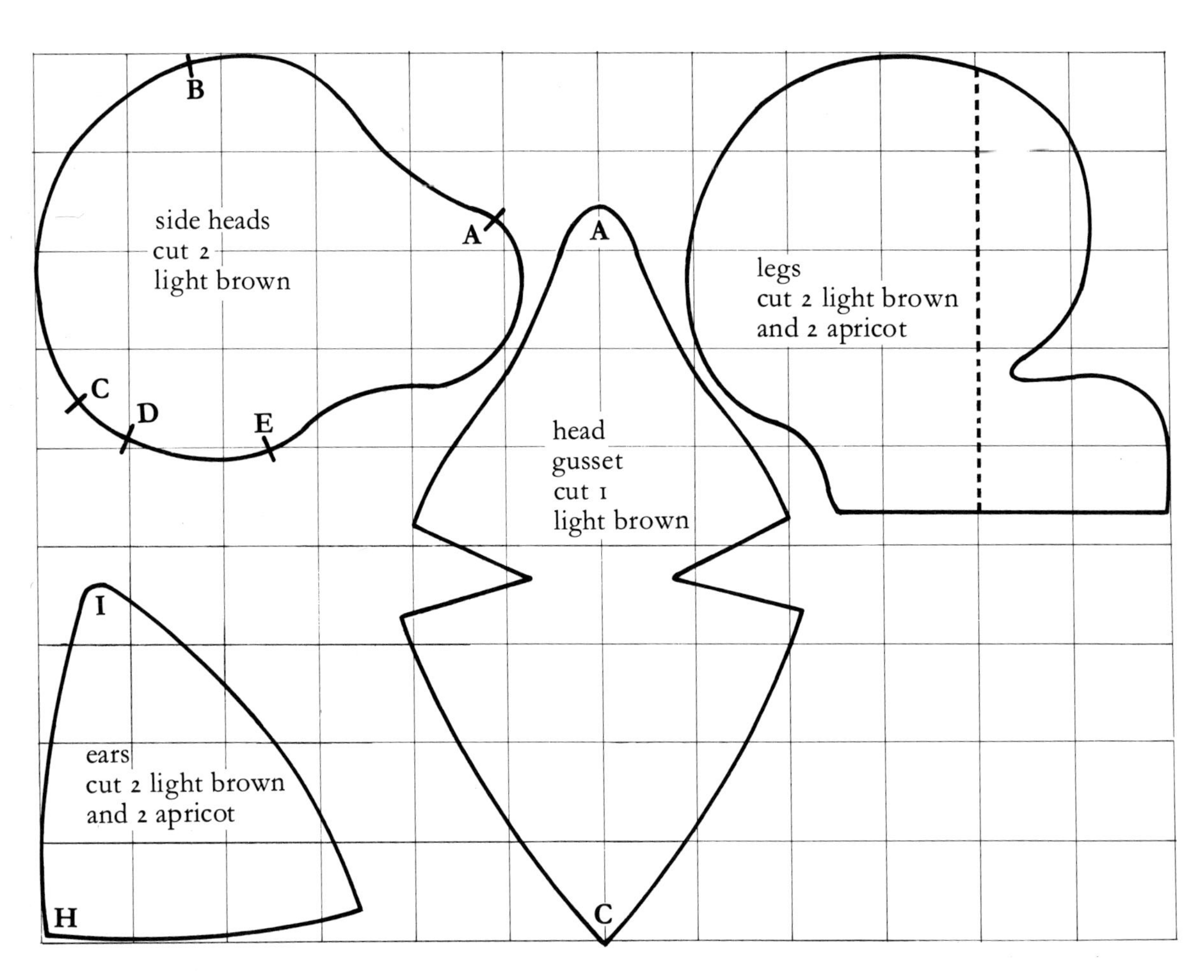

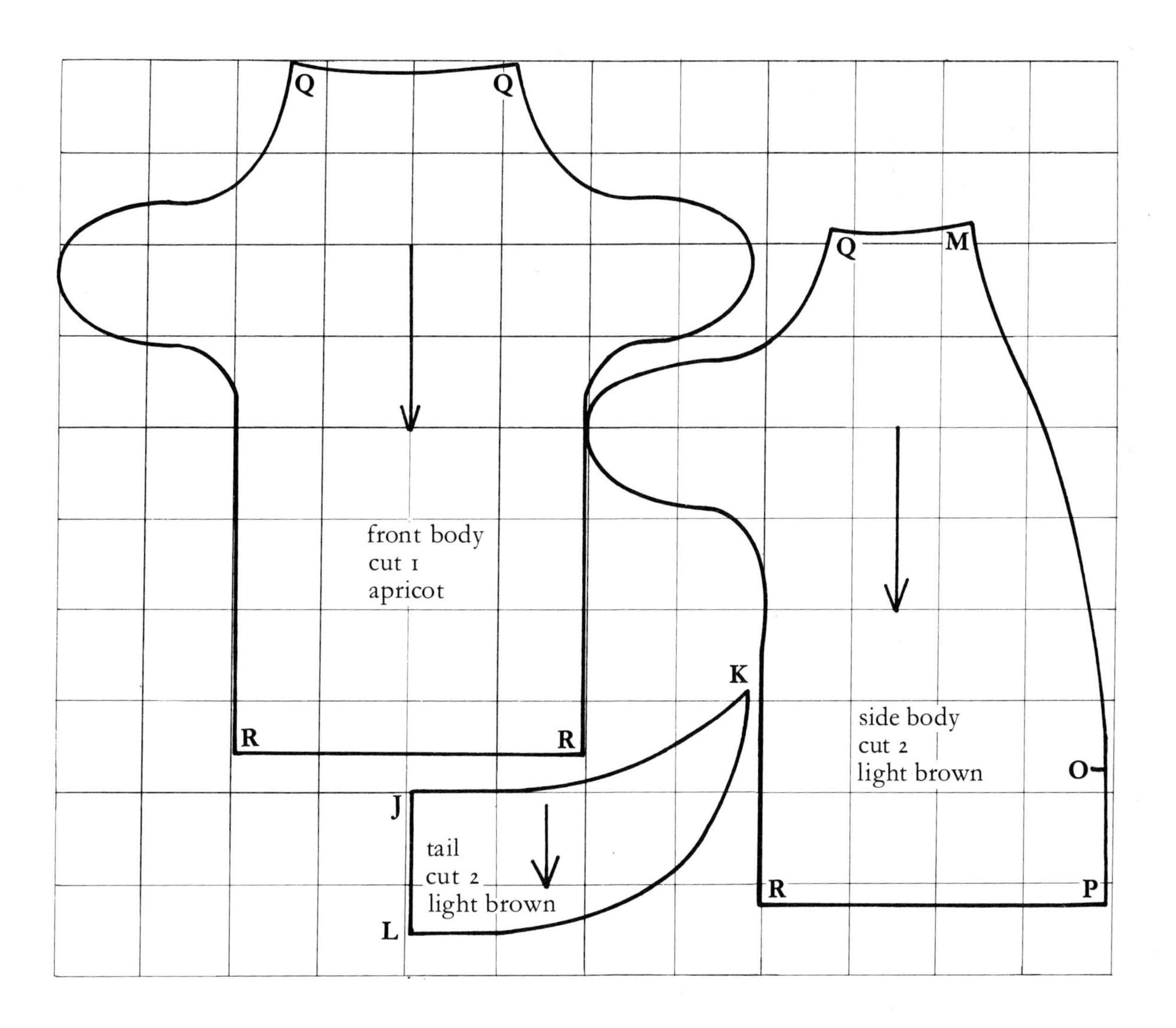

Actual size patterns for Mother

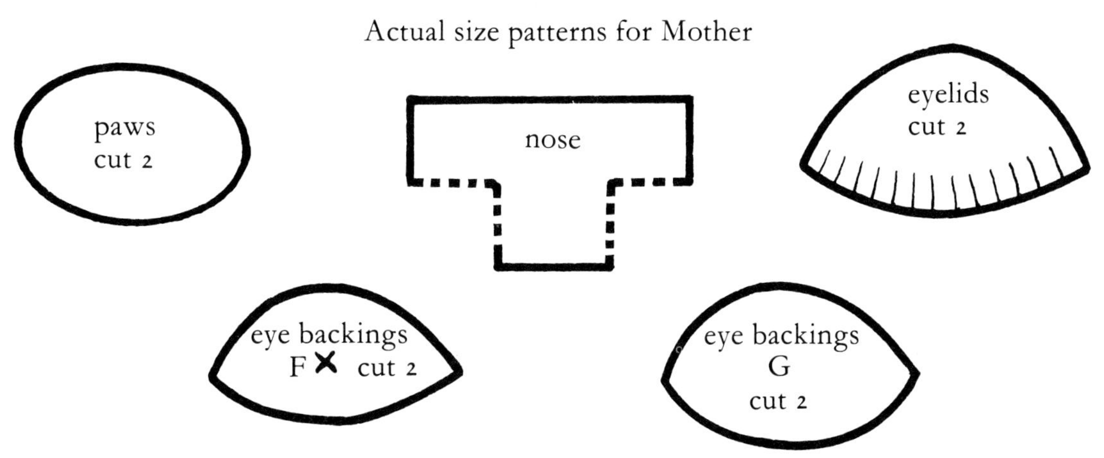

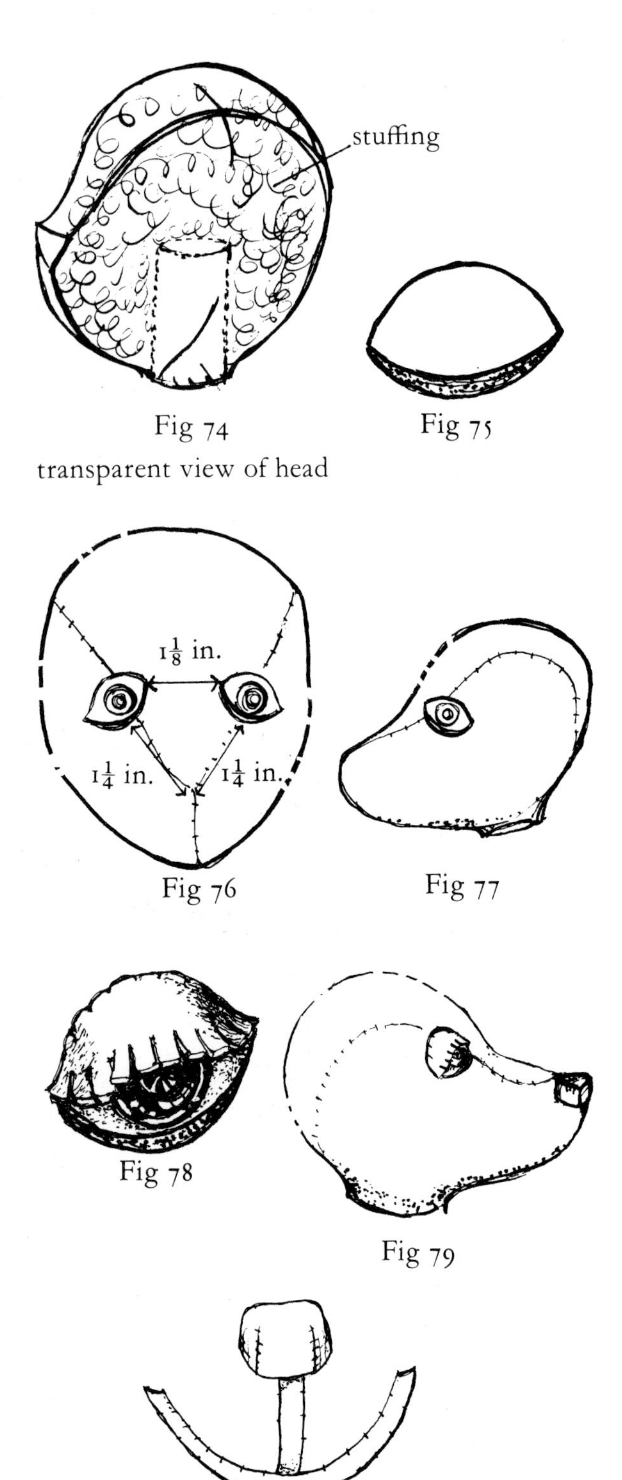

Fig 74
transparent view of head

Fig 75

Fig 76

Fig 77

Fig 78

Fig 79

Fig 80

Head

Cut 2 side heads and one head gusset from light brown material. Mark A, B, C, D and E with tacking threads on the side heads. Close the darts on the gusset. With right sides together, pin A and C on the gusset to A and C on one side head, and pin the gusset dart to B. Oversew lightly in place, taking a $\frac{1}{8}$ in. seam; then back stitch the same distance from the edge. Join the other side head to the gusset in the same way.

Now sew the side heads together from A to E and from C to D for the front and back seams. E to D is left open for the controlling inner tube.

Turn work to right side. Stuff the head with kapok, but before completing roll the thin card along its length to fit the forefinger loosely, stick it together, and push well up into the head. Complete the stuffing and then oversew the neck opening to the lower end of the tube. See fig. 74.

Features

Actual size patterns for the nose, eye backings and eyelids are given on page 47.

Eyes Cut 2 eye backings F from mid brown felt. Cut 2 eye backings G from dark brown felt, and stick them behind the mid brown ones so that dark lower rims will show (fig. 75). Poke a hole with scissor points through the eye backings at X, push the shanks of the glass eyes through, fasten and sink them into the head as described in the introduction. See figs 76 and 77 for the position of the eyes. The eye backings will lie over the seam of the gusset and there should be a distance of about $1\frac{1}{8}$ in. between them.

Cut 2 eyelids from apricot felt and snip into the edges for $\frac{1}{4}$ in. to fringe them into eyelashes. Pin the eyelids over the eyes so that the corners coincide with those of the eye backings; stitch the curved upper part lightly down. Smear some fabric adhesive under the felt, and pad the eyelids with a little kapok to give a rounded appearance and lift the eyelashes off the glass eyes.

Nose Cut the nose from dark brown felt and join the squared edges shown by the broken lines. Place the nose on top of the pointed end of the head, and stitch in place, after padding it firmly.

Mouth Cut 2 strips from dark brown felt $2\frac{1}{2}$ in. and $\frac{3}{4}$ in. long, each approx. $\frac{1}{4}$ in. wide. Pin the shorter one vertically under the nose, and the longer under it in a curved mouth. Stitch down lightly.

Ears

Cut 2 apricot ears and 2 light brown ears, remembering to reverse the pattern to make 2 pairs. With right sides together oversew and then backstitch an apricot ear to a brown ear, leaving the lower edge open. Turn to right side. Oversew the straight edges together. H to I is the inner edge of each ear. Ladder

stitch the ears to the top of the head to cover the gusset darts. The base of the ears should be arranged in a curve and there should be a distance of about $1\frac{3}{4}$ in. between the two ears.

Body

Cut a front body from apricot material and 2 side bodies from light brown, remembering to reverse the pattern pieces. With right sides facing join the centre back seam; but leave the bottom $1\frac{3}{4}$ in. open (O to P).

Cut a centrally placed horizontal slit in the front body $1\frac{3}{4}$ in. wide and $2\frac{1}{2}$ in. up from the lower edge. Oversew its edges to prevent fraying. With right sides facing pin the front body to the back bodies and sew from R as shown on the pattern all round the paws to Q. Do the same on the other side. Turn to right side. Oversew the lower edge to prevent fraying.

Cut 2 mid brown paws from the actual size pattern given.

Tail

Cut 2 tails from light brown material, remembering to reverse the pieces. Place them right sides together and oversew the edges, then backstitch $\frac{1}{8}$ in. from the edge, leaving the straight edge open. Turn to right side. Fold 3 pipe cleaners to fit inside the tail, or use suitable wire; insert and stuff round the stiffening. Close end. Pin the tail into the centre back opening and working from the wrong side oversew the edges of the tail and the side bodies together. Close the remainder of the centre back seam. If the tail droops slightly it will need a stitch or two from the top of its base to the centre back seam to lift it a little.

Shape Lower Back

Tie a knot in one end of the piece of round elastic. Turn the work so that the wrong side of the back faces you. Oversew the knot to the lowest point of one side seam. Fold the edge of the back to the inside for $\frac{1}{4}$ in. and stitch down a narrow hem, at the same time enclosing the piece of elastic. Pull up the elastic so that the back is gathered up to $5\frac{1}{2}$ in., cut off the surplus and oversew the end to the other side seam.

Pocket

Cut a 4 in. square of apricot material and turn a $\frac{1}{4}$ in. hem to the wrong side of 2 opposite sides. Oversew the other edges to prevent fraying. Pin the pocket over the front body so that one hemmed edge is even with the front lower edge, and the sides touch the side seams of the front and back bodies. Oversew in place, leaving the upper edge open.

Legs

Cut a pattern for the legs from the squared diagram on p. 46. Cut 2 apricot legs and 2 light brown legs, remembering to reverse the pattern to make 2 pairs. Run a line of tacking stitches down each apricot leg as shown by the broken line on the pattern. With right sides together oversew and backstitch an apricot leg to a light brown leg, leaving a gap of about $1\frac{1}{2}$ in. on the back curve to turn work to the right side. Stuff the foot part of the leg firmly, and the rest of the leg rather more lightly. Close the gap. Place the tacked line on the apricot inner leg to the side seam of the front and back. The top curve of the leg should coincide with the top corner edge of the pocket. Pin the leg in place from the inside of the body; then with double thread backstitch from a to b as shown on fig. 83, still working from the inside of

Fig 81

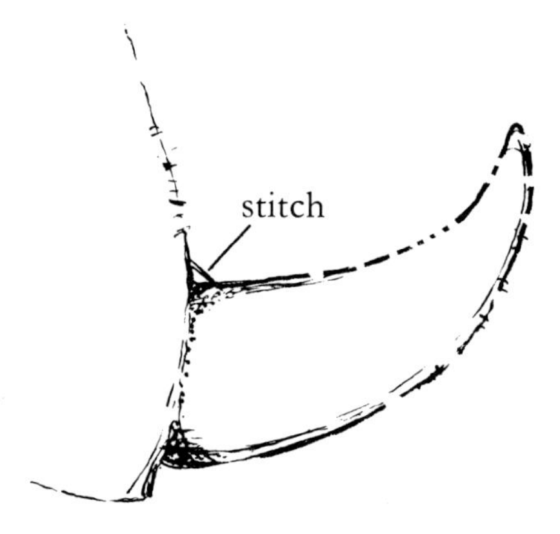

Fig 82

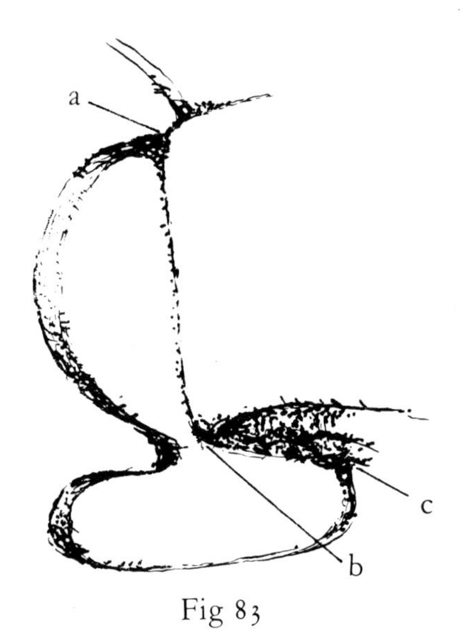

Fig 83

the body. Oversew the gathered back edge of the body to the inner leg from b to c. The back curve of the leg should also be held in place by a line of back-stitches worked from the inside from c round to a again. Sew the other leg to the body in the same way.

Attaching the Body to the Head
Turn a narrow hem round the neck opening of the body to the inside, and ladder stitch the body securely to the head.

To Make Baby
(or Joey, to give him his correct Australian title.) Actual size pieces for the baby are given on this page.

Body
Cut an apricot and a light brown body. Place right sides together and oversew firmly, taking a very small seam, less than $\frac{1}{8}$ in., if you can manage it. Do not backstitch, as this would make the seam too cumbersome. Leave the lower edge open. Turn to right side and oversew the lower edge to prevent fraying. Cut tiny oval paws from mid brown felt and stitch to fore arms.

Head
Cut head pieces from light brown material; with right sides together sew gusset to side heads, matching J and K. Sew the rest of the side heads seam, leaving L to M open for the neck. Turn to right side. Stuff head. Put the forefinger of your left hand into the body and pull the head down over your finger tip, oversew head to body.

Cut 2 ears from light brown material, reversing the pattern pieces and 2 ears from apricot felt. With right sides together oversew apricot ears to light brown ones, turn to right side. Oversew straight edges together. Sew to top of baby's head, with the straighter inner edges facing each other, in a similar position to the mother's ears.

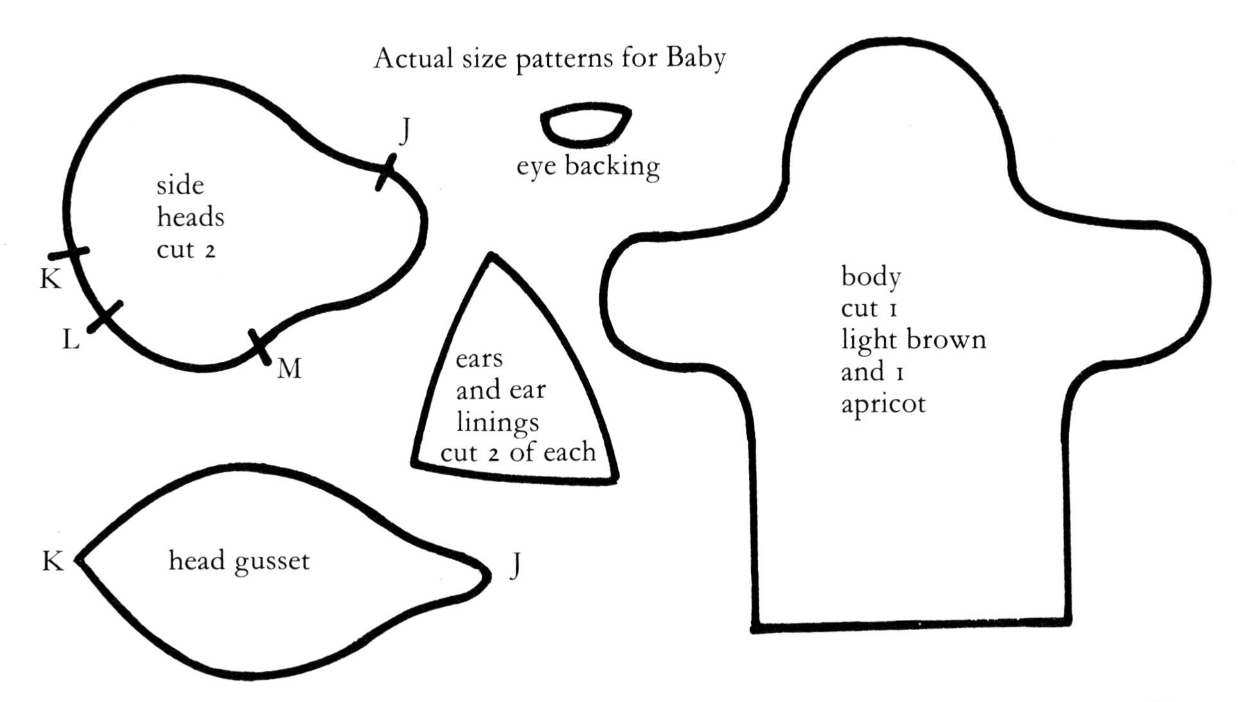

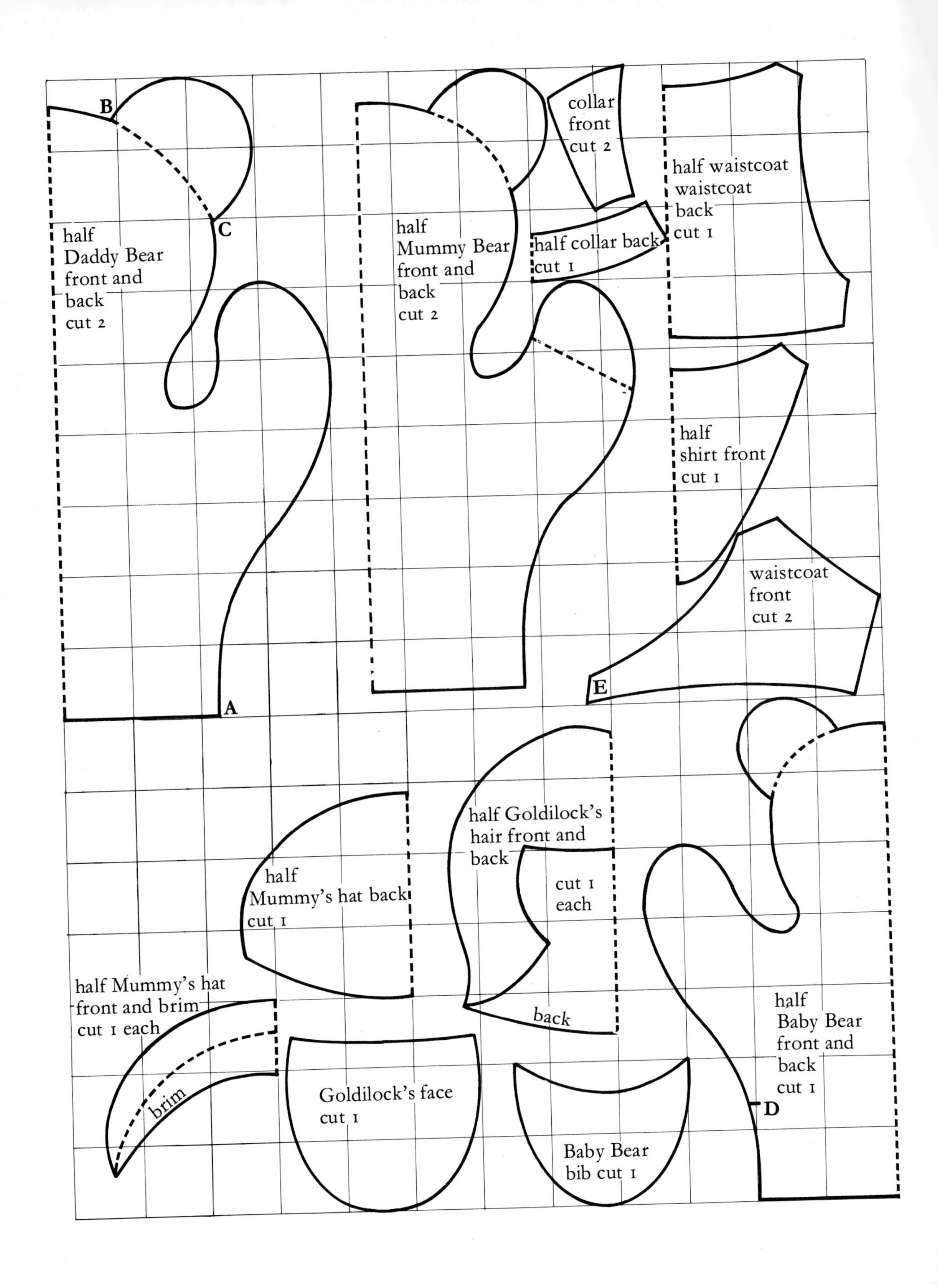

B
C
half
Daddy Bear
front and
back
cut 2
A
half
Mummy Bear
front and
back
cut 2
collar
front
cut 2
half collar back
cut 1
half waistcoat
waistcoat
back
cut 1
half
shirt front
cut 1
waistcoat
front
cut 2
E
half Goldilock's
hair front and
back
cut 1
each
back
half
Mummy's hat back
cut 1
half Mummy's hat
front and brim
cut 1 each
brim
Goldilock's face
cut 1
Baby Bear
bib cut 1
half
Baby Bear
front and
back
cut 1
D

from the edge gives a smart finish, but neat oversewing may also be used. If you are machine stitching start with Daddy first. Begin at lower edge A and sew all round the paw to upper ear point B; reverse direction and stitch back to lower ear point C; following the dotted line as shown on fig. 101: reverse again and stitching into the same holes as far as possible go back to B. Carry out the same technique with the other ear to give more definition to the head. Mummy is stitched in the same way.

Baby needs to be left open at the lower side edges to accommodate the hand. Begin machine stitching at point D on the squared diagram and finish at the corresponding point on the other side. If you are oversewing by hand, back stitch across the ears at their bases.

To Finish Daddy

Cut the collar pieces and the shirt front in white felt. Stitch shirt front in place; cut $4\frac{1}{2}$ in. of fancy braid and cut or turn in the ends at one end to form a point. Cut $1\frac{1}{4}$ in. more braid and sew round the top to suggest a knot. Sew the tie to the centre of the shirt front. Oversew collar back and fronts together at the sides; turn so that oversewing is on the inside and catch centre fronts together over the tie; stick back collar in place. Cut waistcoat back and fronts from red felt; point E is the shoulder on the front. Oversew shoulder and sides; turn oversewing to the inside: edge stitch by machine with black thread or work a small running stitch all round to decorate. Put on puppet over tie and catch fronts together with a small black button or bead sewn on top.

To Finish Mummy

Cut front and back of Mummy's devastating cloche hat from mauve felt. Now cut the pattern for the front along the dotted line shown in the diagram to give a pattern for a narrow brim. Oversew this neatly to the front along the lower curved line. Snip a few small flowers from orange felt, and leaves from dark mauve felt, and stick to one side of the brim; intersperse with small beads. Pin the back and front to Mummy's head, allowing the ears to project as shown in the illustration. Oversew the remainder of the upper edge together, at the sides and between the ears.

Arrange the narrow braid round the neck and let one end hang down; if a strip of fur can be used so much the better. String a necklace and catch it to either side of the neck.

To Finish Baby

Cut Baby's bib from white felt, embroider 'Baby' at the bottom and a few flowers in lazy daisy stitch with french knots for centres and buds, surrounded by leaves also in lazy daisy stitch. Stick the white bib to

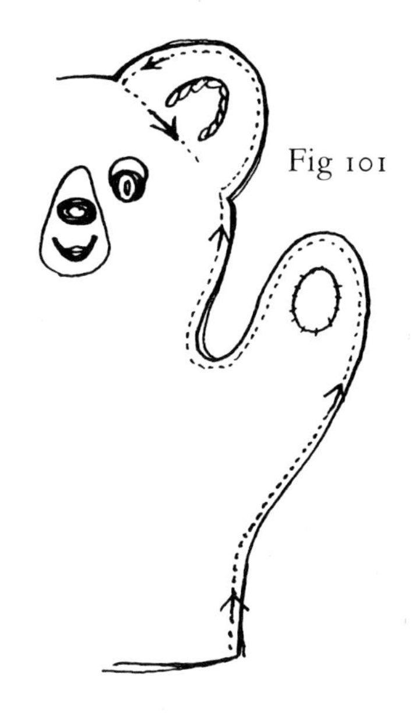

Fig 101

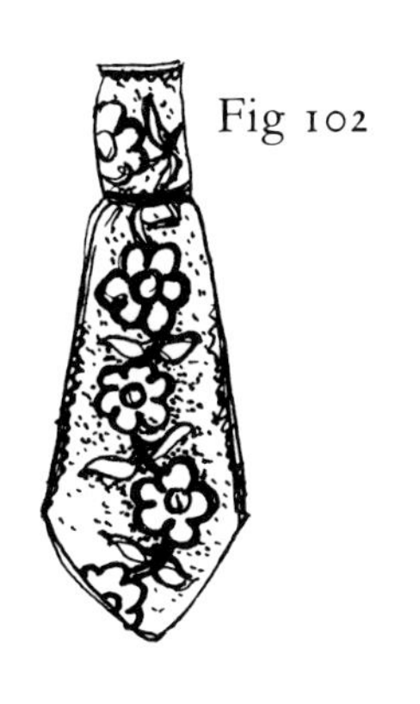

Fig 102

Fig 103

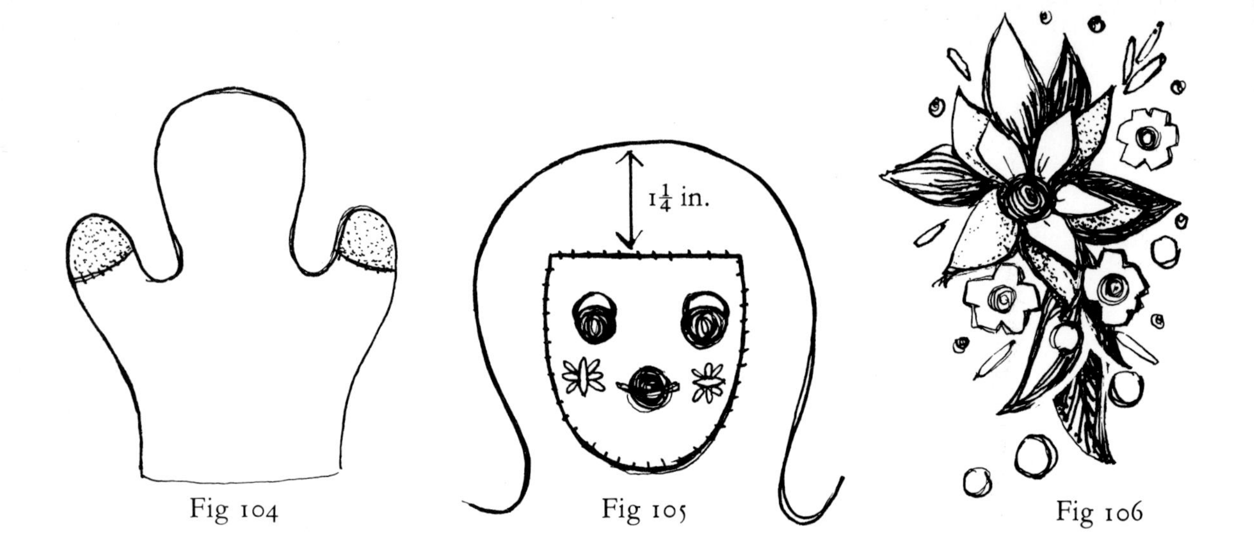

Fig 104
Fig 105
Fig 106

yellow felt and cut round the edge with pinking shears if possible, so that a rim of yellow will show round the white. Attach long narrow yellow felt strings to the corners to fasten the bib round the neck. From the remaining felt cut a bow $1\frac{3}{4}$ by $\frac{3}{4}$ in. and a narrow strip to wrap round the centre; stitch to the top centre of the head.

Goldilocks

Take the pattern for Mummy and cut off the ears at the dotted line shown in the diagram. Cut along the fore arms also at the dotted line. The part which has been cut off will give a pattern for the hands. Cut one back and front from turquoise felt following the altered pattern. Cut 4 hands from pink felt. Oversew the straight edges of each hand to the straight edges of each arm. This oversewing should be on the inside of the puppet.

Cut the face from pink felt and oversew to the right side of the front about $1\frac{1}{4}$ in. down from the upper edge. Add eyes as for Mummy and Daddy bear from white and brown felt. The mouth is a $\frac{5}{8}$ in. circle of red felt, applied across the centre with 2 or 3 red stitches. The cheeks are an embroidered star of 4 stitches in red thread.

Sew a length of braid, ric-rac or frilling down the centre front. Ornament it with 3 or 4 small buttons if liked. Sew a similar trimming round the join of each hand to the arms; turn the edges to the inside.

Cut a small bouquet of felt flowers and stick to the left hand side of the front, or embroider them.

Tack the front to the back, wrong sides together, and edge stitch all the way round by machine or hand oversewing.

Cut the back and front hair from yellow felt; oversew neatly together on the right side all round the outer edge. Fit the hair on the head so that the fringe just covers the top of the face; stick in place.